Anti-Racism

by Byron X Black

About the Author

Byron X Black is a senior coach at Mindset Mastership, a life coaching business based in London, England.

Mindset Mastership teaches clients how human behavior really works. Through our teaching, we have helped clients worldwide gain a better advantage, to develop themselves and achieve more from life.

For further details, see:
MindsetMastership.com

Want free goodies?

Email us at:

mindsetmastership@gmail.com

Find us on Instagram!

@MindsetMastership

Dedicated to you, hoping you'll do the right thing to end racism worldwide

Table of Contents

Introduction

There is racism and racist policy in every region across the globe. Racist acts vary from the use of inappropriate expressions to excluding minorities from jobs and housing as well as other forms of abuse, like physical abuse and even killings. No racial or ethnic group is safe from such virulent acts and behavior. Perhaps there is no better way to counter anti-prejudice activities than by teaching children and young people about prejudice and ways to combat it. After all, racism is just as good as its advocates and practitioners; and trying to educate the next generation is certainly among the best ways to reduce the number of racists and their appeal. This book defines the scope of racist activities worldwide. Many include national or international governments; some are charities and other organizations with private initiatives. Most involve teacher attitudes as reflected in their learning activities while yet others involve the treatment of various cultures within the framework of the school. It is important to keep in mind that these are just a few notable examples – just a few – of traditional racist practices that exist in the community. The subsequent, and much shorter, portion of this study is devoted to explaining a number of websites that communicate, in whole or in part, details about anti-racism to children and young people. But these attempts reflect only a miniscule proportion of current anti-racism reform interventions. While wide variety of informal education and other programs by youth organizations is committed to the battle against racism, it is happening in ever-increasing numbers. It is beyond the reach of this book to explain them in the depth they deserve. Rather, it resides for another day and another study to perform this mission. Looking at the overview, the goal of all considered initiatives is to educate children and young people about racism and prejudice, to equip them with enough awareness to combat and refute prejudice and its faulty theories, and to instill respect for differences between individuals. Ultimately, the book aims at creating a bond of collective tolerance, respect and understanding of others to ensure that they'll never become racists and that racism in others must not be tolerated.

Chapter 1:
Race

The fact that people in America and around the world vary physically in certain noticeable ways is definitely obvious. The most noticeable difference is skin color: some individuals have very dark skin and some have very light skin. Some people have very curly hair, while others have straight hair. Some have thin lips and others have broader lips, just like some people's body features can be different in size and shape as compared to others. At one point, scientists defined as many as nine races, using such physical distinctions as their criteria: African, American Indian or Native American, Asian, Australian Aboriginal, European (more generally referred to as "white"), Indian, Milanese, Micronesian, and Polynesian (Smedley, 1998).

While people certainly do vary greatly in physical characteristics, it has led to the creation of racial categories. Anthropologists, sociologists, and many geneticists have since assessed the effectiveness of these categories and therefore the value of the biological concept of race (Smedley, 2007). It is clear that inside a given race we often see more physical differences. Some Europeans have bright and light skin while others have a darker complexion, such as those from some Eastern European backgrounds. Some "whites" actually have darker skin than some "blacks," or African Americans. A few white people have very straight hair while others have very curly hair; some have blue eyes and blonde hair yet others have dark hair and brown eyes. Due to interracial relations that go back to the days of slavery, African Americans often vary in their skin's darkness and other physical characteristics. It is estimated that approximately 80% of African Americans have white (i.e. European) ancestry; 50% of Mexican Americans have European or Native American ancestry; and 20% of whites have African or Native American ancestral roots. If racial disparities once existed hundreds or thousands of years ago (and many scientists deny these disparities once existed), such distinctions have become more and more blurred in today's world.

A further reason to question the genetic idea of evolution is that an individual or group of people is often assigned to a social class for arbitrary or even irrational reasons. For example, a century ago, Irish, Italians, and Eastern European Jews who left their native lands to go to the United States for a better life were not considered as white upon arrival, but seen as different (Painter, 2010).

Take into account any African American with a set of parents and you will see these parents are two distinct races. What kind of race is this person? Usually, white America calls a person black or African American, yet the person may not have the same identity (like Barack Obama, who had a white mother and father from Africa). Think about the reason for this? Imagine someone as the offspring of one black parent, one white parent and perhaps one brown grandparent. So, this individual has three genetic races: parents white and one grandparent black and one mixed. Since this person's ethnicity is only 75 percent white and 25 percent black, he or she is likely to be considered black in the United States and may very well accept this cultural identity. This practice reflects the conventional "one-drop rule" in the U.S. which recognizes somebody as black if they have at least one iota of "black blood" that was used to keep the institution of slavery as high as possible in the antebellum South (Wright, 1993). If we look at this practice in the United States, about 80 percent of people we call "black" will now be called "white." A racial term should have better coverage in terms of social norms rather than mere biological aspects.

A third reason to doubt the scientific conception of race comes from the biological field itself, more precisely from genetics and human evolution studies. Beginning with genetics, in their DNA, people of different races are more than 99.9 percent the same (Begley, 2008). To switch this around, less than 0.1 percent of all the DNA in our bodies allows for the physical differences we associate with racial differences. People having different backgrounds do have social similarities while they may be dissimilar in biological aspects.

Race as a social construct

Racial groups are classified on the basis of biological differences. Another way of saying this is that race is a social invention, a term that doesn't possess objective truth but, instead, is what people agree it to be (Berger & Luckmann,

1963). From this perspective, race has no material existence other than what and how people think about it.

This view is represented in the issue of placing people with multicultural backgrounds in any one racial category, as highlighted earlier and as seen in the example of President Obama. As another example, when he exploded onto the golfing scene in the late 1990s, the famous (and now notorious) golfer, Tiger Woods, was usually labeled as an African American in the media, but in fact his ethnicity is half Asian (divided equally between Chinese and Thai), one-quarter white, one-eighth Native American, and just one-eighth African American (Leland & Beals, 1997).

Past precedents of attempts to place individuals in racial groups further underline racial social constructionism. The skin color of slave labor softened over the years during the time of slavery in the South as children were born out of the union, mostly in the form of rape, of slave owners and other slave whites. As it was impossible to say who was "black" and who was not, there were plenty of legal fights over ethnic identity. Individuals convicted of black descent had to go to court to prove they were white to avoid enslavement or other problems (Staples, 1998). Susie Guillory Phipps sued the Louisiana Bureau of Vital Records in the early 1980s which is a fairly recent example of changing one's official ethnicity to white. Phipps descended from a plantation master and white ancestors. Previously, she had thought of herself as white and was shocked to find out that she was legally black after seeing a copy of her birth certificate, though she had one black ancestor about 150 years ago. She lost her case, and so did the United States. Later the Supreme Court refused to revise it (Omi & Winant, 1994).

While race is a societal construct, as noted earlier, it's also true that things perceived as real are indeed real in their consequences. It’s actually happening. Seeing as very little of DNA accounts for the physical distinctions that we equate with racial differences, even a small amount leads us not only to divide people into various races but also to treat them differently – and more to the point – unequally on the basis of their classes. Yet modern evidence shows that there is little, if any, empirical justification for the classification of races that has been the cause of so much injustice.

Chapter 2: History of Slavery

African tribes were captured and carried to work in the Americas, the UK, and other colonial countries. The ample land "discovered" in the Americas was useless, without enough labor to exploit it, according to European colonial officials. Structures of labor exploitation favored slavery, but neither European nor Native American origins were sufficient enough for this task.

The trans-Saharan slave trade had long supplied African enslaved labor to work in Mediterranean sugar plantations alongside Russian and Balkan white slaves. This same trading also sent as many as 10,000 slaves a year to serve masters in

North Africa, the Middle East, and the Iberian Peninsula. Having proven themselves skilled workers in Europe and on nascent sugar plantations on the Madeira and Canary Islands near Africa, enslaved Africans were the labor market of choice in the Western Hemisphere — so much so that they were the vast majority of the colonial populations of the Americas.

Of the 6.5 million slaves who survived the Atlantic crossing and settled in the Western Hemisphere between 1492 and 1776, about one million were European citizens. The remaining population of five and a half million were African. An average of 80 percent of these Africans were enslaved people—men, women, and children employed mostly as field workers. Both women and children served. Just very young children (under six), the aged, the sick and the infirm escaped enslavement.

More than approximately half of these enslaved African were employed on US sugar plantations. Sugar became the leading commodity produced by slaves in the Americas. Brazil dominated sugarcane manufacturing during the 16th and 17th centuries. One of the oldest large-scale manufacturing industries was founded to convert the sugar cane juice into sugar, molasses, and eventually rum, the triangular trading alcoholic beverage of choice.

Interestingly, the profits from the sale of these products in Europe and the trade in these goods in Africa were used to buy more slave labor. Saint Domingue (Haiti) overtook Brazil as the leading sugar producing colony during the 18th century. The number of slaves brought to Haiti's tiny island was more than double the number smuggled into the US. But the Haitian Revolution outlawed slavery and led to the creation of the first black republic in America. Consequently, Haiti 's supremacy over world sugar production was brought to an end.

Cuba assumed that role throughout the 19th century, and in the 20th century, even after slavery was abolished in 1886, sugar remained the pillar of its major export commodity. Sugar was also produced by slaves on the other Caribbean islands, and also in Louisiana in the United States.

During the United States colonial era, tobacco was the dominant resource produced by slaves. Tobacco plantations largely focused in Virginia and Maryland used the highest proportion of enslaved Africans prior to the revolution period of America. The American Revolution lost Virginia and Maryland to the key European tobacco markets, and the future of slavery in the United States was in doubt for a brief time after the Revolution. It was abolished by most northern states, and Virginia also debated emancipation in the Virginia Assembly.

The 1793 cotton gin invention gave slavery new life in the U.S. From 1800 till 1860, the cotton produced by slaves spread from South Carolina and Georgia to the newly colonized lands west of the Mississippi region. This shift from the upper south to the lower south of the slave economy (Virginia and Maryland) was followed by a similar shift of the enslaved African population to the lower south and west. Just after end of slavery in 1808, the key cause of expansion of slavery into the lower south was internal slave trade. The overwhelming majority of enslaved Africans employed in plantation farming were field hands. They did other work on the plantations. Some were housekeepers and worked as butlers, waiters, maids, seamstresses and laundries. Some were allocated to be drivers of carriages, hostlers, and stable boys. In addition, artisans — carpenters, stonemasons, blacksmiths, millers, coopers, spinners, and weavers — were also hired as part of the labor force.

Enslaved Africans were also employed in urban areas. In the United States, ten percent of the enslaved African population lived in the cities. Charleston, Richmond, Savannah, Mobile, New York, Philadelphia and New Orleans had sizeable populations of slaves. They totaled roughly a third of the population in southern cities.

In towns, the range of slave occupations was vast. It was governed by domestic servants, but there were carpenters, fishermen, coopers, draymen, sailors, masons, bricklayers, blacksmiths, bakers, tailors, peddlers, painters, and porters. Since many worked directly for their owners, others were appointed to plantations, public works projects, and industrial enterprise as skilled laborers. A small proportion hired themselves out and asked to pay their owners a percentage of their profits.

Every plantation economy was part of a bigger domestic and foreign political economy. The financial model of cotton plantations, for example, is generally seen as part of the American South's regional economy. In fact, "cotton was king" in the South by the 1830s. It was also the king of the United States, competing in world political theory for economic leadership. Planting cotton formed the basis of the southern economy of the antebellum era (occurring or existing before the U.S. Civil War).

But the American financial and shipping industries, too, relied on cotton provided by slaves. So did the textile industry in

Britain. Cotton was not sent from the South straight to Europe. It was instead transported to New York and then shipped to England and other cotton production centers in the United States and Europe.
As the cotton plantation system spread throughout the Southern region, New York's banks and financial houses supplied loan and/or investment capital to buy land and slaves. Africans were appointed as an inexpensive source of labor and became crucial economic and political assets in American politics and economics. Enslaved Africans were a type of property – a commodity, legally. They were frequently used individually and collectively as collateral in all sorts of business transactions. They were also traded for goods and services.

Sometimes, the interest from the slaveholders' investments in their slaves was used to acquire loans to buy additional land or slaves. Slaves were often used to pay off unpaid debts. When estimating the value of estates, the approximate value of each slave was included. A huge tax revenue was generated by local and state governments. Taxes were levied on slave transactions too.

Politically in the United States, the Constitution incorporated a characteristic that made Africans enslaved political capital for the benefit of southern states. The so-called three-fifths agreement allowed southern states to count their slaves as three-fifths of an individual for the purpose of determining the number of states in the U.S. Committee. Therefore, the power balance between slaveholders and non-slaveholders turned partly on the existence of the three-fifths of enslaved Africans in the census. Slaveholders were taxed on the same three-fifths principle, and the national treasury was not supported by any tax payable on slaves. In short, the U.S. system of slavery was a regional practice that touched the very core of its society and politics.

Institutional and wealth development

By some estimates, New York received 40% of US cotton revenue; its financial firms, shipping businesses and insurance companies earned money through African slavery. A line can be drawn between slavery and modern economic practices in the U.S. and the UK. People in non-slave areas - Britain and the free U.S. states - routinely did business with slave owners and engaged in slave commerce. But the “uniqueness” of slavery's economic contribution has been "exaggerated."

Slavery thrived under colonial rule. British and Dutch settlers relied on enslaved people to help establish farms and build new towns and cities that would eventually become the United States. Enslaved people were brought to work on cotton, sugar, and tobacco plantations. The crops they grew were sent to Europe or to the northern colonies to be turned into finished products. Those finished goods were used to fund trips to Africa to obtain more slaves who were then trafficked back to America. This triangular trading route was profitable for investors.

To raise the money to start many future plantation, owners turned to capital markets in London - selling debt that was used to purchase boats, goods, and eventually African slaved people. Later in the 19th century, U.S. banks and southern states would sell securities that helped fund the expansion of slave-run plantations. To balance the risk that came with forcibly bringing humans from Africa to America, insurance policies were purchased.

These policies protected against the risk of a boat sinking, and the risks of losing individual slaves once in America. Some of the largest insurance firms in the U.S. - New York Life, AIG, and Aetna - sold policies that insured slave owners would be compensated if the slaves they owned were injured or killed. By the mid-19th century, exports of raw cotton accounted for more than half of U.S. overseas shipments. What wasn't sold abroad was sent to mills in northern states, including Massachusetts and Rhode Island, to be turned into fabric.

The money southern plantation owners earned couldn't be kept under mattresses or behind loose floorboards. American banks accepted their deposits and counted enslaved people as assets when assessing a person's wealth. In 2005, JP Morgan Chase, currently the biggest bank in the U.S., admitted that two of its subsidiaries - Citizens' Bank and Canal Bank in Louisiana - accepted enslaved people as collateral for loans. If plantation owners defaulted on loan payments, the banks took ownership of these slaves.

JP Morgan was not alone. The predecessors of Citibank, Bank of America and Wells Fargo are among a list of well-known U.S. financial firms that benefited from the slave trade. Slavery had an overwhelmingly impact on the American economy. While cities like Boston never played a large role in the slave trade, they benefited from their connections to slave-driven economies. New England merchants made money selling timber and ice to the south and the Caribbean. In turn, northern merchants bought raw cotton and sugar.

New England's fabric mills played a key role in the U.S. industrial revolution, but their supply of cotton came from the slave-reliant south. Brands like Brooks Brothers, the oldest men's clothier in the country, turned southern cotton into high-end fashion. Domino's Sugar, once the largest sugar refiner in the U.S., processed slave-grown sugar cane. America's railroads also benefited from money earned through slave businesses. In the south, trains were built specifically to move agricultural goods farmed by enslaved people, and slaves were also used as labor to build the lines.

Deaths, trauma, and the torture of slaves

In the United States, the handling of slaves varied by time and place but was generally harsh, especially on plantations. Whipping and rape were common, but usually not before white outsiders or even the relatives of the plantation owner. ("When I whip niggers, I take them out of the vision and sound of the house, and no one in my family knows it".) A slave could not give testimony against a white woman; slaves were sometimes required to whip other slaves, even relatives. There were times when a slave owner could turn over the whacking.

The southern picture on slave treatment

The following declaration was prepared on the occasion of the arrival of "the seditious and insurrectionary proceedings of a

Fanatical Society in New York, which purported to send some of its superstitious, dumb, and filthy publications to Frederica's (Georgia) post office" at a respectable meeting of the inhabitants:

"Our slaves enjoy the most ideal security and freedom from excessive labor, the most unlawful riots and violence, so often inflicted on the North Blacks. Consequently, the state of our slaves is [sic] implicitly more autonomous, comfortable and safe than those overburdened and marginalized workers, who are dressed and fed— Have just as much land as they can develop — raise up an abundance of poultry, interchange for comforts and some of the luxuries of life; and when the sick or the afflictions of a faithful old age secure for them such liberty that the hypocrites and religious zealots of this abolition mania will never afford them, their desires are supplied and carefully attended in a comfortable hospital on most of the plantation. It is his pleasure to see them happy. Such are the relationships between master and servant, and these vile abolitionists, these conflicts, and anarchists will sever [sic], And these are the positive people they want to cast into a wide and pitiless world unprovided!!"

Brutality

The treatment of slaves was harsh and inhumane according to historians David Brion Davis and Eugene Genovese. Slaves suffered physical abuse during work and outside of it since it was allowed by the government. The treatment on large plantations was usually harsher, often managed by overseers in lieu of the absent slaveholders. Some slave owners even worked with their slaves and sometimes handled them in more humane manner. Including massively overworking, the slaves endured brandings, massacres, "floggings" and even worse punishments. Flogging was a term used to describe a slave 's daily lashing or whipping for misbehavior.

Inhumane treatment

After 1820, some slave owners enhanced the living conditions of their slaves in reaction to their inability to legally import new slaves from Africa following the ban of the foreign slave trade, to persuade them not to try to escape. Some advocates for slavery claimed many slaves were satisfied with their situation. African abolitionist, J. Sella Martin, argued that the obvious "contentment" was in fact a psychological shield against the dehumanizing cruelty of having to bear witness to the selling of their spouses at auction and the raping of daughters. Likewise, Elizabeth Keckley, who grew up in Virginia as a slave and became a personal modist of Mary Todd Lincoln, gave an account of what she had seen as a child to illustrate the foolishness of any suggestion that a slave was cheerful or happy. In the account, Little Joe, the cook 's son, was sold to pay toxic loans to his owner.

Working conditions

In 1740, after the Stono Rebellion, Maryland restricted the working hours of slaves to 15 per day in the summer and 14 in the winter, with no work allowed on Sunday. Charles Johnson, a historian, argues that these laws were motivated not only by sympathy but also by the need to pacify slaves and avoid possible revolts. The employment environment of slaves was often aggravated by the need for the plantation to sustain itself with regard to food and shelter.

Punishment and abuse

Slaves were thus punished with whipping, shackling, hanging, beating, burning, mutilation, branding, rape, and jailing. Punishment was sometimes committed in reaction to defiance or suspected crimes, but often violence was used to reassert the master's (or supervisor's) authority. Knives, weapons, field tools and other items were used on them. The whip was the most popular device wielded against a slave. One said, "Whipping was the only punishment I ever heard or knew of being prescribed to slaves," although he knew several who were beaten to death for offenses like "sassing" a white person, hitting another "negro," "squabbling" or quarter fighting.

The most repeated punishments were imposed on slaves who worked and lived on plantations. Such penalties might be imposed by the owner or manager of the plantation, his wife, children or (most frequently) the inquisitor or operator.

Let's look at a modern example of racism.

Nazi anti-Semitism and the Holocaust

Throughout Germany, the whirlwind of anti-Semitic aggression loosed by Nazi Germany under Adolf Hitler's leadership from 1933 to 1945 not only reached a frightening peak but also motivated anti-Jewish campaigns elsewhere. The Cagoulards (French for "hooded men"), the Arrow Cross in Hungary, the British Union of totalitarians in England, the German-American Bund and the Silver Shirts in the United States enacted racism and xenophobia rampantly. Anti-Semitism in Nazi Germany managed to reach a level never encountered before. Centuries ago, Christianity had sought the persecution of Jews, and political leaders from Spain to England had mandated their removal. The Nazis later found Jews not only to be members of a subhuman group but to be a deadly disease that would kill the German people, so the party sought the "final solution to the Jewish problem," in the form of the assassination of all Jews, males, females and children. The eradication of the Jews was crucial to racial filtration and even the redemption of the German people in Nazi ideology, which perceived Jewishness to be biologically inferior.

A novelty of the Nazi brand of anti-Semitism is that it crossed the boundaries of gender. The Aryan idea of racial superiority appealed to the masses as well as to the economic elite. Anti-Semitism in Germany became national policy that was required to teach, postulated in "scientific" books and advocated by educational institutions and newspapers that endorsed this international disinformation. In 1941, European Jewry to be liquidated was part of official party politics. Approximately 5.7 million Jews were hunted down and killed by mobile killing units during the Second World War and placed in death camps such as Auschwitz, Chelmno, Belzec, Majdanek and Treblinka, where they died from hunger and gassing.

Chapter 3: The effect of World War II on Migration

Global waves of immigration have grown in volume, thereby shifting in character since the end of World War II. From 1945 to the early 1970s, large numbers of foreign workers were drawn from various colonial nations to the rapidly-developing industrial areas of Western Europe, North America, and Oceania. The oil crisis of 1973-74 marked the end of this period. These migrants may be classified into three large groups: (1) migrants from the European periphery to Western Europe, mostly by "guest-worker systems;" (2) ethnic migrants from the former colonial powers and (3) regular migrants to North America and Oceania, first from Europe and later from Asia and Latin America.

European migrants at the end of the Second World War (the most significant refugee movements in Germany after 1945) were a political force. They consisted of returning migrations of former settlers to their country of birth as territories gained independence. World War II enormously affected migrants all over the globe.

Guest workers' in Western Europe

The German government began actively recruiting guest workers during the latter half of the 1950s in response to a labor shortage triggered by high rates of economic growth. Germany signed a number of bilateral agreements with Italy, Spain, Greece, Turkey, Morocco, Portugal, Tunisia, and Yugoslavia, enabling refugees to temporarily work in industries that need both unskilled and skilled labor. Under the guest workers agreement, foreign workers were to go back to their home countries and be replaced by new ones once their contracts had expired. However, in practice many foreign workers stayed permanently in Germany. This was in line with the interests of employers, who preferred to continue with their older staff, and the workers' attitudes themselves; they came to see Germany increasingly as their home and many decided to take advantage of the greater prospects for income. The recruitment of foreign labor from all non-EC countries was halted in 1973 as a result of oil shortages and the subsequent economic recession in the early 1970s. Nevertheless, the ban allowed many foreign employees to live indefinitely in Germany, because it would have been more difficult or even impossible for them to return briefly to their home countries and then come back to Germany. The influx of immigrants from former guest worker nations in the subsequent years consisted mainly of the relatives of those guest workers who managed to stay in Germany (family reunification).

While the German “guest worker” system is well known, all the rapidly industrializing Western European countries used the temporary hiring of labor at some stage between 1945 and 1973, as the rapidly expanding economies were able to make use of the less developed European periphery's labor reserves. Austria and Switzerland saw the large-scale import of labor, with employers hiring foreign workers from abroad. The governments regulated entry and residency. Relaxation on family gatherings and permanent stay contributed to the development and settlement of migrant communities. In 1945, France set up an Office National immigration (ONI) to organize the hiring of Southern European workers.

Migration was seen as a solution to the shortages of labor of the post-war period and what the French called their "demographic inadequacy." Huge family settlement was envisaged in the light of ongoing low birth rates and casualties from war. Belgium also began hiring foreign workers soon after the war. They were mainly Italian citizens, working in coal mines and in the steel and iron industries; however, others took in their dependents and eventually settled down.

In the 1960s and early 1970s, the Netherlands and nearby lands also brought in "guest workers," such that Luxembourg industries, for example, was heavily dependent on foreign labor. Sweden employed workers from Finland and Southern European countries. In the 1960s, Italy witnessed internal migration from the underdeveloped south to the northern industrial triangle between Milan, Turin and Genoa, which became very close in social and economic character to the international labor movements in other European countries. Though guest workers were recruited in Britain shortly after the Second World War, the system was fairly limited and short-lived, since the use of colonial staff was simpler (as discussed below).

Colonial workers

While "guest workers" were non-residents and seen as temporary employees, supposed to leave after several years, colonial employees were citizens of their former colonial power or had some special right to join and stay in it. They were generally entitled to civil and political rights and most intended to remain permanently.

For Britain, France and the Netherlands, the migration from the old colonies was significant. Between 1946 and 1959, Britain saw inflows from Ireland, its traditional reserve of labor, providing manual labor for manufacturing and domestic use. Many took their families with them and settled permanently. In Britain, the Irish enjoyed all existing civil rights, such as the right to vote.

The entry of New Commonwealth workers nearly stopped after 1962, partly because of the emergence of strict limits and partly because of the early onset of economic instability in the UK. However, most of the immigrants from the Commonwealth had come to stay, and family reunification continued until 1971. France witnessed large-scale immigration from its former colonies, especially from Algeria, Morocco, and Tunisia, but also from the former colonies of

Senegal, Mali, and Mauritania in West Africa. Some of these migrants had come before independence, although remaining as French residents. Others came later through favorable migration provisions. There were two major inflows from former colonies in The Netherlands: "repatriates from the former Dutch East Indies (now Indonesia) entered the Netherlands between 1945 and the early 1960's. After 1965, a growing number of workers from Suriname's Caribbean territory came to the Netherlands.

Permanent migration to North America and Oceania

Because of restrictive legislation introduced in the 1920's, large-scale migration to the U.S. happened later than in Western Europe. The 1965 reforms to the Immigration and Nationality Act were regarded as part of the period's civil rights legislation, intended to abolish the unequal quota system for national origin. These amendments created a global immigration system, where kinship with U.S. citizens or residents was the most important criterion for admission. The outcome was a spectacular upsurge in Asian and Latin American migration. US employers also recruited temporary migrant workers, mainly men from Mexico and the Caribbean, especially in agriculture.

After 1945, Canada adopted mass immigration policies. Although only Europeans were admitted at first, after 1966 the implementation of a non-discriminatory "point system" for screening prospective migrants opened the door for non-European migrants. In the 1970s, Jamaica, India, Portugal, the Philippines, Greece, Italy, and Trinidad were the principal destinations. Entry was supported over time, and migrants were seen as potential settlers and citizens.

After 1945, Australia launched a mass immigration program, as policymakers believed that the populace needed to increase for both economic and geopolitical reasons. The strategy was one of continuous family immigration, summed up in the famous slogan "populate or perish."

A common characteristic of the 1945-1973 migratory movements is the preponderance of economic motives. Migrations of foreign workers to Western Europe were mainly triggered by economic factors on the part of refugees, employers, and the governments. The same holds true for the recruitment of contract staff for U.S. farming. Economic motives played a major role in Australia's post-war migration program, although consideration was also given to population building.

There were generally economic reasons for the colonial workers who migrated to Britain, France, and the Netherlands, although political concerns (such as the wish to maintain links with the former colonies) also played a role for these governments. Permanent migration to the U.S. was definitely the movement with the least influential economic force. But the migrants themselves also had economic motives, and their labor played a significant role in the development of the U.S. economy. The largely economic reason for migration in the post-1973 period is less clear-cut.

Another key result of the period between 1945-1973 was the increasing diversity of the areas of origin and the increasing cultural disparity between the migrants and the recipient countries. In the beginning, most refugees came from different parts of Europe to the major receiving countries. As time went on, Asia, Africa and Latin America saw rising proportions. This pattern was to become much more pronounced.

Anti-Semitism

Anti-Semitism is any hostility to Jewish people as a religious or racial group, or discrimination against them. In 1879, The German activist, Wilhelm Marr, invented the phrase anti-Semitism to explain the anti-Jewish protests currently taking place in central Europe. Although the term now has broad circulation, it is a misnomer, because it implies bigotry against all Semites. The Arabs and other groups are also Semites, but as is generally believed, they are not the target of anti-Semitism. The term is particularly improper as a label for the prejudices, declarations, or actions of Arabs or other Semites against the Jews. Nazi anti-Semitism, ultimately resulting in the Holocaust, had a homophobic dimension in that it targeted Jews because of their supposed genetic features — even those who had converted to other religions or whose parents were converts. This form of anti-Jewish bias stems back from the rise of so-called "scientific racism" in the 19th century and is distinct in origin from previous anti-Jewish biases.

The anti-Semitism in and outside Europe since the Holocaust

Anti-Semitism lost the support in Western Europe and the United States for a stretch after the 1945 Nazi surrender. Only those who were anti-Semitic would refuse to show it, if not ashamed. Post-war, American Jews were an integral part of culture and society. Hurdles to Jewish involvement in business and politics fell by the wayside, and as Jews sought to participate in American life, they found few obstacles in their way. Anti-Semitism is a marginal phenomenon of today's hate crimes, with occasional lethal manifestations. But even if they were less numerous, less pervasive, and less tolerated by American society, there are still infrequent virulent anti-Semitic acts.

In several other nations, however, anti-Semitism has continued. Soviet dictator, Joseph Stalin, whose soldiers had liberated Auschwitz, participated in a purge of Jews that was only stopped by his 1953 death. Opposition to the State of Israel after the Six-Day War (1967) and efforts by Soviet Jews to emigrate from the Soviet Union is linked to historical Russian anti-Semitism.

John XXIII and the Second Vatican Council, under the guidance of the Pope (later Saint), the Roman Catholic Church recognized Judaism 's validity as a continuing religion and found Jews innocent for the assassination of Jesus Christ by universalizing blame for his crucifixion. *Nostra aetate* is probably the most influential text in twentieth-century Christian-Jewish relations; the Good Friday liturgy was updated to make it less contentious with regard to the Jewish people, and the Roman Catholic catechism was modified. However, in 2007, Pope Benedict XVI approved the wider use of the old Latin mass, which included the liturgy of Good Friday and a prayer that most Jews deemed objectionable.

Although the prayer was revised to deal with Jewish concerns in 2008, some argues that it is still injurious.

The fight against anti-Semitism and the acceptance of Jews was a centerpiece of the papacy of Pope John Paul II, who witnessed the Holocaust directly as a young man in Poland. The pope paid a landmark visit to a synagogue in Rome in 1986, and under his guidance, the Vatican formed diplomatic ties with the State of Israel in 1993, shortly after the end of the Israeli-Palestinian Liberation Organization Oslo peace accord. The pontiff visited Israel in March 2000. He defined anti-Semitism as anti-Christian in the natural world and absolved Christians for anti-Semitism at Yad Vashem, Israel's Holocaust memorial. He put a note of prayer of forgiveness for past Christian wrongdoings in the Western Wall, the holiest place of Judaism:

"We are profoundly saddened
by such behaviors
who in history
have caused yours children to suffer,
and seek forgiveness.
We want to get engaged
for true fraternity
to the Covenant of Men."

The Vatican published a document entitled, "We Remember: A Reflection on the Shoah" in 1998, calling on believers to reflect on the Shoah's (Holocaust) lessons. In introducing the text, Edward Idris Cardinal Cassidy, Chairman of the Commission for Religious Ties with the Jews of the Holy See, said, "Whenever there is remorse on the part of Christians, this responsibility should be an appeal to repent."

Although the collapse of the Communist bloc in the early 1990s and the improvement in the teachings of the Roman Catholic Church and other Christian denominations about the Jews might have dealt a massive blow to anti-Semitism, global disputes over Nazism's legacy in Austria and Switzerland have triggered increased anti-Semitism in those countries during the 1980s and 1990s. Global outrage about Kurt Waldheim 's Nazi past caused a violent anti-Semitic response amongst his supporters after his stunning victory for Austrian leadership in 1986.

In the late 1990s, when it was made public that Swiss banks had embezzled Nazi gold during World War II (most probably confiscated from Jews) and failed to return the money to Jewish borrowers after the battle, international criticism, and requests for compensation from Switzerland led to increased anti-Semitism. Political opponents in post-communist Russia to the ruling regime and to the unequal power of Jews among the powerful oligarchy often had anti-Semitic overtones.

In addition, the creators of Zionism and the members of the Israeli government believed that the Jewish situation was standardized — that is, the accomplishment of statehood with a flag and an army — would significantly diminish anti-Semitism. Indeed, from the Yom Kippur War of 1973 onward, the presence of the Israeli state seems to have had the opposite effect, fueling rather than quenching the anti-Semitic fires. Accordingly, in the first days of the millennium, there seemed to be a marked increase in anti-Semitism. In Europe it was assumed that the emergence of a large Muslim immigrant community profoundly concerned with events in the Middle East would exacerbate anti-Semitism.

The most insecure Jews living in immigrant communities were the victims of anti-Semitic acts. It was argued that the large number of Muslim immigrants and the lack of legislation on hate crimes led some European politicians to disregard or downgrade the importance of anti-Semitic incidents. In addition, despite the anti-Semitic myths that Western Europe had thrown away in the post-Holocaust era, such as the procedures of the Learned Elders of Zion and the blood libel, anti-Semitism still found its way to the gulf region where, with the help of religious leaders, the press and some government bodies, they thrived. While some commentators argued that Islam was not anti-Semitic by definition, the Muslim world held currents of intensely anti-Israel and actively anti-Semitic views while abroad.

Islamic societies tolerated Jews as people of the book and dhimmis for many centuries, subordinate but covered citizens, who had to pay special taxes, wear identification clothes, and stay in different areas. Thus, the Jews were treated much like other unbelievers in Muslim societies. But the immigration of large numbers of Jews to Palestine in the twentieth century and the formation of the State of Israel (1948) in a former Arab region stirred new currents of animosity within the Arab world. Because Arabs are Semites, they are primarily political (or anti-Zionist) and religious rather than ethnic in their hatred of the State of Israel. However, whatever the reason, the result has been the adoption of several anti-Jewish initiatives across the Middle East Muslim countries. In addition, most of those countries' Jewish citizens immigrated to Israel in the decades that followed its establishment.

However, the ferocity of the wrath and threats against Israel seemed not to differentiate between Israelis and Jews. Armed attacks have both been aimed at civilian and military targets.

Some of those alarmed by rising 21st-century anti-Semitism have pointed to examples of Muslim leaders using anti-Semitic clichés when discussing their own communities. Around the same period, the Internet united fragmented groups of anti-Semites and created a formerly segregated online platform for factions.

Other factors appear large in the analysis of what was portrayed in the Western media as the "new anti-Semitism." Especially, a major part of the political left became strongly critical of Israel in many countries, a trend that was alarming to Jews who were once on the left and thought that their former allies had turned against Israel or its policies. Some opponents of these policies contrasted them with those of Nazi Germany, and Jewish figures were portrayed in political cartoons in a manner not unlike Nazism. Simultaneously, many conservative Christians (including many evangelicals) expressed ardent support of Israel. However, in the countries like Greece and Hungary, the far-right nationalists who are xenophobic – often symbolized by open or barely disguised anti-Semitism while looking to capitalize on economic distortion and unhappiness at immigration – received greater political power.

Anti-Semitism scholars and students have failed to make a distinction between the rational criticism of Israeli government policies and true anti-Semitism. In 2004, then Israeli cabinet minister and former Soviet human rights activist, Natan Sharansky, proposed three markers to delineate the border between rational criticism and anti-Semitism. Within his 3D scheme, when one of the components was observable, the line had been crossed: dual standards (judging Israel by one criterion and all other countries by another), delegitimization (the assumption that Israel has no right to exist), or demonization (considering the Israeli state not simply as wrong-headed or misguided, but as a supernatural power in the contemporary world).

Civil rights

Civil rights guarantee gender equality and social-legal protection, irrespective of race, religion, or other personal attributes. The existence of civil rights legislation has led to the growth of minorities in a state or country. Human liberties include voting rights, the right to equal jury, the right to public care, the right to education and the right to use public amenities. Democratic rights are an integral part of democracy; when people are denied opportunities to become active in democratic life, their democratic rights are violated.

Unlike civil liberties, which are rights secured by imposing limits on government, civil rights are protected by the meaningful intervention of the government, often in the form of law. Civil rights laws seek to guarantee fair and effective citizen status to persons traditionally discriminated against on the basis of certain group characteristics. When many find the enforcement of civil rights inadequate, a civil-rights movement may emerge to call for equal the enforcement of existing rules without discriminatory practices as seen in the rage against racism in the U.S. police force.

Unlike other definitions of freedom, such as human rights or natural rights, in which citizens naturally obtain rights either from God or nature, civil rights must be granted and protected by the power of the State. Consequently, they vary with cultures and forms of government; they tend to follow sociological theories that condone or abhor specific forms of discrimination. For example, the civil liberties of the lesbian, gay, bisexual, transgender, and queer (LGBTQ) minority in some democratic nations have only recently moved to the forefront of political discourse.

The civil rights movement in United States of America

The Civil Rights movement in the United States had its roots in a campaign to end discrimination against African Americans. Though slavery had ended and political rights were legally given to former slaves after the Civil War, African Americans continued to be routinely disenfranchised and exempted from modern society in the majority of Southern States, such that they have become lifelong second-class citizens. By the 1950s, African American marginalization had sparked an epic social revolution, sometimes taking an incredibly violent turn. The Movement for American Civil Rights was located predominantly in African American churches and campuses in the South included marches, boycotts, and widespread civil disobedience campaigns, including lay-ins and voter literacy and voting campaigns. Most of these attempts were local, but the effect was felt at the national level as a model of civil rights organization that has since spread throughout the world.

The global-based civil rights movement

The diocesan priest-led progressive movement in Northern Ireland during the 1960s was influenced by its ties to the

United States. Its initial focus was on combating discriminatory gerrymandering, which had secured elections for Protestant unionists. Later, both a mass protest campaign and the more progressive techniques of the Irish Republican Army (IRA) sparked the internment of Catholic activists by the British government bodies, leading to vicious sectarian strife (1968–1998).

A high-profile civil rights movement has brought an end to the South African racial segregation system known as apartheid. A rebel group started in the 1940s and escalated in the 1950s and '60s, when civil rights were hitting the globe as a philosophy, but it was pushed underground as most of its members were incarcerated; it did not regain power until the 1980s. Diplomatic pressure associated with internal upheaval eventually resulted in lifting the ban on the African National Congress, South Africa's main black party and Nelson Mandela's release from prison in 1990. Mandela later became South Africa's first black president in 1994.

The civil disobedience and social mobilization of the Dalits in India is a more recent movement with striking parallels to both the American civil rights movement and the South African struggle against apartheid. The Tamils, previously known as "untouchables" and now officially Scheduled Castes, make up around one-sixth of Indians. They were compelled to remain as second-class citizens for years, and many were not even considered to be part of India's varna network of political hierarchical structure. Dalit activism, such the efforts of Bhimrao Ramji Ambedkar, led to great successes including Kocheril Raman Narayanan's election as president. The fact that India's leader is elected by parliament, whose members once came predominantly from the upper castes, shows how much the mindset has changed.

In addition to such globalization, many groups in the U.S. have been inspired by different levels of success of the American Civil Rights Movement in fighting for more government protections. Most importantly, women have made strides in the field of job rights, having acquired the right to vote in 1920 through a constitutional amendment. Until now, the women's rights movement has stopped just short of the Equal Rights amendment, which would codify women's equal rights in the U.S. Constitution. Constitution. Since its failure to be accepted in 1982, women have seen numerous changes in court rulings that ruled against sex discrimination and have witnessed the passage of laws such as the 1991 Civil Rights Act, which set up a commission to examine the existence of the "glass ceiling" that has stopped women from rising to top management roles on the job.

Since the 1960s, several other groups have been the focus of civil rights movements. The U.S., the Congress national party approved the Indian Civil Rights act in 1968. Latinos and Asian Americans campaigned for expanded civil rights based on a history of ethnicity, religion, language, and immigrant identity discrimination. Multi-lingual education reforms and legacy admissions program started to mount. More recently, Arab Americans and the LGBTQ community have taken center stage in the fight for equal rights and equal opportunities in American society. Following the terrorist attacks of September 11, 2001, Arab Americans have experienced increased rates of bigotry and hate crimes, forcing them to adhere to government policies that limited their freedoms, as codified in the infamous U.S PATRIOT Act of 2001.

In the late 1990s and early 2000s, the gay rights movement made big strides. Some countries allow same-sex marriage and others give same-sex civil partnership advantages; but at the dawn of the twentieth century, the majority of the U.S. population opposed same-sex marriage. In addition, several U.S. social conservatives have proposed a constitutional amendment banning marriage between the same sex. However, by 2010, about half of the U.S. population favored the legalization of same-sex marriage, and in its 2015 Obergefell decision on the June v. Hodges case, the Supreme

Court ruled that laws banning same-sex marriage were unlawful; under due process and the Fourteenth Amendment's sovereign immunity clauses, thus ultimately legalizing same-sex marriage in all fifty states.

Nearly all countries have deliberately refused the human rights of ethnic or population groups. Since civil rights are practiced in various countries, an international standard for civil rights security is difficult to create, despite the efforts of international governance organizations like the U.N. The international human rights law, ratified by the General Assembly of the United Nations in 1948, protects the terminology of civil liberties but is not enforceable on national governments. Civil rights continue to increase as governments feel pressure to enact reforms, either from political protests or from other countries.

Racial segregation

Racial segregation is the process of limiting access to certain residential neighborhoods or separatist institutions (e.g., schools, churches) and facilities (parks , playgrounds, restaurants, restrooms) on the grounds of race or alleged race. Racial segregation provides a means of preserving the financial rewards and dominant social standing of the politically dominant majority and until recent times, the white population has been intent on sustaining their superiority over other classes by means of legal and cultural color bars. Historically, however, different conquerors — including Asian Mongols, African Bantus, and American Aztecs — have also practiced prejudice in the form of race separation.

Segregation has reared its ugly head in all parts of the world where there are multiethnic societies, except in Hawaii and Brazil, where racial assemblage occurs on a large scale. There has been sporadic racial inequality in many countries while not a formal segregation. Of note, from the late 19th century to the 1950s, legal segregation in public amenities was upheld in the southeastern United States. (See Jim Crow legislation.) In the 1950s and 1960s, Southern blacks initiated the civil rights movement to rent asunder the machine of racial segregation. This movement fueled the passage of the 1964 Civil Rights Act, which contained strong anti-discrimination and segregation provisions in voting, education, and public use. Racial segregation was conducted elsewhere with a great degree of rigor in South Africa, where it was official government policy under the apartheid regime from late 1950s to the end of 1990.

Chapter 4: Race And Ethnicity

Race and related theories related are widely debunked today (Miles, 1989). There are, of course, bodily human differences such as facial tone, and genetic variation between people from various parts of the Earth. "What is wrong is the assumption that these are the foundations of discreet human racial groups with cultural and ethical features based on their biological differences." But the narratives and processes of racism persist. "Racialization" is a central principle in this respect. It corresponds to "the social process of granting cultural importance on such visible evidences and, as a rule, to impose them under the system of injustice." Even though the notion of racialization has ultimately been used in a weak and ambiguous manner (see Murji & Solomos, 2005), it efficiently describes the path of meaning granted to organizations and exclusive methods. Today, the fundamentals of race and racism are intertwined with animosities generated by the racialization of migration, religious beliefs, and country discourse. Many engaged in racializing narratives are eager to escape the accusation of bigotry, which plays to the idea that we survive in a post-racial world. The word "race" and the notions associated with it "have a significant historical affiliation with advanced racialized enslavement, colonization domination and political and financial marginalization."

The challenges brought on by anti-racial thought have prompted others to accept the concept of nationality as a "general term from which 'race' concepts can be taken as a subset." The definition of race "means the way in which sociocultural distinctions, language and heritage converge as a component of social activity and social organisation and form a systematically repeated classification structure." We can see five main categories of circumstances in which race forms an significant part self identity: when urban minorities are created by migration, when tribal sub-national communities are established who reject and claim their own nationality, between long-term minorities in multicultural societies, when native minorities are deprived by colonial settlement, and between posts. This renders the subject very complex, maybe too complex, but several scholars have come to see ethnicity as much more critically beneficial and more benevolent than race. So it is fair to see race as far less rooted in suspect terms. There are also cases in which ethnicity is racialized and/or related to the same patterns of injustice that define the history of race.

Economic development in the western world cannot be properly understood without taking into consideration race and gender and their relationship to colonialism. Cultural development is also directed at disseminating, integrating, and commercializing essential aspects of culture from the outskirts of society. Combined with the racialized perception of creativity and legitimacy, this can have a powerful impact on cultural development. For this and other causes, cultural development theorists need to make the interconnected oppressions associated with race and ethnicity much more important than they have been to date — and these oppressions must also be hypothesized in comparison to the power structures of class, gender, as well as other influences.

Toward a more Integrated Approach

Studies provide a significant vision into the process of race and ethnicity. However, few attempts have been devoted to integrating such perspectives into a more unified method of race and ethnicity. The argument is that we need more coherent solutions to solve some of the issues noted above, in particular the requirement for a higher level of clarification and analysis of general innovations and changes.

A selection of attribute describes an effective holistic approach:

- A comprehensive approach to incorporate macro-and micro-explanations and viewpoints. In general, an interpretation of social evolution must focus on a contextual view of the unique and complex forms that society and cultural life take in various societies. The admiration of these distinctions would require effort in terms of industrial development and the appropriation of cultural values. This should not, however, contain a philosophical bent in which Western trends of industrial development and commodification are seen as the probable outcome of "less developed" communities. Empirical evidence requires providing an overview of the myriad of financial, social, and cultural ties amid various types of unity, along with the co-existence of "donations" and commodity-based financial relations.

- Acknowledging the multiplicity of types that cultural production may take in various cultures does not exclude the awareness of those specific systemic factors that affect cultural output through different communities, or by the organization of cultural producers and audiences.
- A comprehensive view needs to include definitions of cultural development that consider the several forms of forces that affect life and structures, including physical, socio-cultural, political and technical influences, and their dynamic interplay.
- One must take an historical view, not only in the context of making reference to historical case studies, but also in the context of comprehending how any framework is the outcome of various historical forces. This involves an understanding of the ever-changing and developing existence of cultural development in various communities (along with the inclination towards gradual obsolescence and "entrepreneurialism" in cultures marked by "liberal modernity"). Conversely, it also includes an

> appreciation of the fundamentals underlying continuity. In other words, cultural development must be interpreted as characterized by several temporalities. This helps to prevent simplistic, linear forms of transition (such as those who say that digitization has contributed to a move from an industrial era of cultural development to a digital world).

It would be impossible for any human statistician to completely illustrate all these traits within a lifespan of study, let alone a particular report or book. On some scale, these are the characteristics of research projects premised on a division of work, with researchers involved specific types of analysis. The argument here is that all statistics deeply related to consistent evaluation will have to state clearly their stance on the conceptual and analytical challenges seen in the sub-field (production studies) or focus on new challenges.

In line with any of these circumstances, we now proceed to the next step, first by giving a conceptualization of common cultural production and then describing how such theorization might integrate an evaluation of race and ethnicity.

Chapter 5: Privilege

The concept of white privilege

Privilege, particularly "white privilege" or "white male privilege" is hard to see for born with access to power and resources. However, it is often very visible to those to whom privilege has not been granted. Furthermore, the subject is extremely difficult to talk about because many white people don't feel powerful or feel they have privileges others do not. For those who have privileges based on race, gender, class, physical ability or sexual orientation, or age, it just the norm.

Most of us are clear, however, that people whose skin is not white are members of a race. The surprising thing for us is that, even though we don't see ourselves as part of a radical group, people of color generally do see us that way. So, given that we want to work to create a better world in which all can live, what can we do? The first step, of course, is to become clear about the basics of white privilege, what it is and how it works. The second step is to explore ways in which we can work against the racism of which white privilege is the cornerstone.

White privilege is an institutional (rather than a personal) set of benefits granted to those who, by race, resemble the people who dominate the powerful positions in our institutions. One of the primary privileges is that of having greater access to power and resources than people of color; in other words, purely on the basis of skin color, doors are open to whites that are not open to other people.

Racism vs. white privilege

Basically, racism is what happens when you turn the conviction of privilege into practice. For instance, a person may unconsciously or actively assume colored people are more likely to commit crimes or be dangerous. This is a partiality. If an individual perceives a black person as angry, that person may become nervous. This stems from a bias. These biases become racism through a variety of actions, ranging from individual to group responses:

- An individual runs across the street to avoid a group of young black men walking together.
- An individual calls the police to report a person of color who may otherwise be acting lawfully.
- A policeman is shooting an unarmed black person because "he feared for his life."
- Despite scant evidence, a jury finds a person of color guilty of a violent crime.
- A federal intelligence department prioritizes black and Latino groups to prosecute rather than white nationalist violence.

Racism and bias both depend on what social scientists call racialization. That is a people grouping based on perceived physical differences, including skin tone. Historically, this arbitrary classification of individuals has intensified prejudices and become a tool for justifying the unfair treatment and oppression of non-white citizens. Likewise, the pain, relocation, harsh treatment, and prejudice against people of black color eventually gave birth to white privilege.

White privilege through the years

White privilege is more psychological — a subconscious prejudice perpetuated by the lack of awareness among white people that they hold this power. White privilege may be seen in everyday purchases, and in the willingness of white people to travel fairly freely across the professional and personal worlds. Yet some people of color continue to argue against the aftereffects of deliberate decisions contained in aspect of white privilege. For example, because a lot of people of color are not employed by white business owners, white people have more economic opportunities. The right to retain complex control is, in itself, a white privilege and it endures. Legislative agencies, corporate leaders and educators are often overwhelmingly white and make deliberate decisions (laws, hiring practices, discipline procedures) that iterate this cycle of repetition.

The more complex truth is that white supremacy is practiced unconsciously, and perpetuated consciously. On the surface, it is deeply embedded in American life. It's a weightless knapsack — and a gun.

White privilege as the "power of normal"

Sometimes even the examples used to make white privilege visible to those who possess it are also the least damaging examples for those who lack it. But this does not mean that such examples are trivial or do no harm. Such implicit examples of white privilege are used for people who might fight back against the definition as a convenient, simple entry point. These are easy, everyday things - conveniences that white people are not forced to ponder.

Such examples sometimes include:

- The first aid kit with "flesh-colored" Band-Aids that only matches white people's skin tone.
- White people's hair products are not found in a smaller, separate section of "ethnic hair products" but in the big aisle labeled "hair care."
- The grocery store stocks a variety of food choices that reflect most white people's cultural practices.

Yet sometimes, the origin of such problems is overlooked. These examples can be rejected by white people who might say, "My hair is curly and needs a unique product," or "My family comes from Poland, and it's hard to find traditional Polish food at the grocery store."

This may be true. But the reason for focusing on such basic white privileges is that the harm goes beyond the discomfort of shopping for products and services. Such privileges are indicative of what we might term the "power of normal." If public spaces and amenities appear to cater to one race and divide the needs of citizens of other races into different segments, it might suggest something under the surface.

White people are more likely to travel around the world, expecting their needs to be met readily. Colored people move around the world knowing their needs are on the fringes. To recognize this means knowing that there are differences.

The white privilege as the "power of the benefit of the doubt"

The "power of norm" goes beyond the local CVS. White people are much more likely to see positive representations on television and in films in which the cast looks like them. They are more likely to be viewed as people than as members of a stereotyped racial group (or exceptions to it). To put it another way, they are more often humanized and given the benefit of the doubt. They are more likely to get compassion, to be given individual potential, and to survive errors. This has adverse repercussions for people of color, who face the implications of racial discrimination, stereotyping and a lack of respect for their hardships without this privilege.

White privilege in these scenarios:

- White people are less likely to be pursued by law enforcement if they seem "suspicious."
- The skin color of white people isn't going to be a reason people refuse to trust their reputation or financial responsibility.

- When white people are convicted of a crime, they are less likely to be considered guilty, less likely to be sentenced to death, and more likely to be depicted by media outlets in a rational, complex manner.
- The personal mistakes of white people will probably not be used to reject their opportunities or compassion to those who share their ethnic identity.

To many white people, their privilege is invisible, and it seems fair that a person should be given consideration when they travel around the world. It seems fair that a person should be given the opportunity to prove himself independently before he is judged. Allegedly, it is an American ideal.

But it's still a luxury not provided for people of color — with serious consequences. Those who survive racial profiling — whether subtle or violent — do not escape unaffected. They suffer from post-traumatic stress disorder, and this trauma in turn impacts their peers, families, and local communities, who as a result are vulnerable.

A study conducted in Australia (which has its own hard history of enslaving black and indigenous peoples) strikingly shows how white privilege can appear in day-to-day interactions — a constant reminder that one is not deserving of the same benefit of the doubt granted to those of diverse cultural and ethnic identities. In an experiment, more than 1,500 attempts were recorded of those who tried to board public buses, telling the driver that they don't have enough money to pay for the ride. The results: the driver allowed 72 percent of the white people to stay on the bus. The same empathy was applied to just 36 percent of the black men.

Just as colored people have done nothing to deserve this unfair treatment, white people did not "earn" such access to disproportionate empathy and fairness. They take it as a byproduct of systemic racism and prejudice. And even though they are unaware of it in their everyday routines as they walk down the streets, this privilege is the product of deliberate choices made long ago and choices still made today.

White privilege as the "power of accumulated power"

Maybe the most important lesson on white privilege is the one which has least been instructed. The past subconscious by-products of discrimination are not the only examples of the "power of normal" and the "power of the benefit of the doubt." They are the purposeful effects of racism that allow injustice to recreate permanently. These powers would not exist had it not been for systemic racism coming first. And systemic racism cannot survive unless these powers continue to hold sway.

You can picture it as a loop of whiteness, in which racism is like rain. The rain populates the world, giving more access to life and wealth in some areas than others. Evaporation is white privilege — an invisible idea that is both the rain and the reason it begins to go away. Rather, the difference largely relies on inheritance — wealth transferred from one generation to another. And that richness often comes with value in the form of inherited homes. When white families are able to collect wealth because of their earning power or home value, they are more likely to nurture their children into early adulthood, helping with expenses such as higher education, their first cars and their starter homes. The loop goes on.

This is a right that is denied to many communities of color, a denial that started with the work of state legislators and property managers. After the Second World War, there was woven "a magic middle-class carpet," consisting of discriminatory zoning laws that segregated cities and towns from a significant number of colored people — from Baltimore to Birmingham, from New York to St. Louis, from Louisville and Oklahoma City to Chicago and Austin, and towns beyond and between.

Such exclusionary zoning policies grew like weeds from local codes and the redlining of the Federal Housing Administration (which does not finance loans or those residing near blacks), to more sophisticated methods incorporated into building codes. The result: colored people were not allowed to raise their kids and spend their money in "good home value" communities. Today's cycle continues. Prior to the 2008 crash, people of color were unfairly represented for subprime mortgages. And the diversity of neighborhoods continues to correlate with low property values across the U.S. As per the Century Survey, one-fourth of poor black Americans live in barrios of high poverty; just 1 out of 13 poor white Americans lives in a high-poverty neighborhood.

The inequities are piling up. About 80 percent of poor black students attend a high-poverty school to this day, where suspension rates are often higher and services are scarce. Hurdles remain when out of school. There are still racial differences between economic forgiveness and trust. In a study conducted by the University of Wisconsin, 17 percent of white work applicants with criminal background got a call back from an employer; only five percent of black applicants with a criminal history got a call back. According to the National Bureau of Economic Research, black Americans are 105 percent more likely to obtain a high-cost mortgage than whites, with Latin Americans 78 percent more likely to receive a high-cost mortgage. That is after monitoring factors like credit score and debt-to-revenue ratios.

Why address these issues in a white privilege article? It is because of the income inequality in the past and the current prime examples of white privilege. If privilege refers to laws that affect individuals from other origins, then what is more powerful than a history of laws that has deliberately targeted ethnic minorities to keep them out of communities and deny them access to resources and services?

If white privilege is "to have greater access to power and resources than colored people do," then what is more exemplary than access to land, access to communities, and access to power to segregate towns, refuse loans, and maintain such systems?”

This white privilege example also shows how structural inequities flow down to less harmful forms of white privilege. Wealth inequity contributes significantly to the "power of doubt" whenever a white person receives a lower mortgage rate than a colored person with the same credit credentials. Wealth imbalance reinforces the "power of normal" whenever businesses assume that the white base is their most profitable consumer target, and they adjust their products accordingly.

Citizens may of course be unaware of these inequities. According to the Pew Research Center, just 46 percent of white people say they benefit "a lot" or "a decent amount" from the advantages that society does not offer blacks. But those privileges are conscious choices to uphold, and this goes beyond credit authorities and lawmakers. Numerous studies have shown that many white people endorse the concept of racial equality but are less supportive of measures that might make it more palatable, such as reparations, affirmative action, or law enforcement reform.

In this way, white privilege isn't just the ability to find what you need in a convenience store or travel around the world without defining your experiences by race. It is not just the subconscious comfort to see a world serving you as normal. It is also the power to remain silent when confronted with racial inequity. It is the capacity to complain or discuss the discomforts or inconveniences of speaking about it. White privilege means getting to choose when you want to take a stance and where. You and your dignity are free.

Chapter 6: What is intersectionality

Intersectionality may be regarded as a method of seeing how sociocultural categories are intertwined. It seeks to investigate the relationship between gender, age, religion, disability, orientation, class, and citizenship. The term, intersection, indicates when one line slices across another, which can be used to traverse others' paths. Intersectionality was once defined as a crossroads in the American sense of the term to describe ways in which persons of color cross gender boundaries (Crenshaw 1989). American scholars have been critical of gender-based work for generating gender differences with homogenized ethnicity. Males and females were analyzed as distinct and heterogeneous even within the groupings of males and females in feminist studies. Nevertheless, race-based critiques stated that females and males were all Caucasian and both the same in Western culture when it comes to the issue of ethnicity. The emphasis has been on race and gender in the American notion of intersectionality. Since research cantered on the deprived and oppressed colored people, the analytical perspectives and evaluations also suggested the social aspect (Crenshaw 1995). Disability and sexualities were included in the intersectional paradigm.

The complexity of intersectionality

To apprehend the complexity of intersectionality, American sociologist, Leslie Mc Call, uses 3 approaches: *anticategorical intricacy*, *intracategorical intricacy*, and *intercategorical intricacy* (Mc Call,). Intersectionality is defined as "interactions between numerous levels and modes of cultural relations and particular topic creation." Anti-categorical intricacy is linked to post-structural feminists and to reinterpretation. This intricacy "denies" or impoverishes ethnicity, class, gender, and sexual orientation. Building and demolition of groups is a matter of language.

The main philosophical implication of this strategy has been to make use of classifications, but they have no basis in fact.

Language (in a wider social or conversational sense) generates normative fact instead of the other way around. According to Mc Call, this method compares wisdom and strength by means of exemption and inclusion processes. Anticategorical intricacy can be applied to multiple genders, sexual orientations, sexuality, and multiculturalism in order to prevent fixed and prescriptive structures and disciplines.

Intracategorical ambiguity is related to color feminism, and McCall positions this strategy between anticategorical and intercategorical strategies. An intracategorical strategy is introduced to explore cross-categories and identities and can concentrate "on specific social classes at overlooked points of intersection." Observers are crucial to a particular use of groupings. They are crucial to broad and sweeping classification actions instead of being crucial to classification per research. This strategy is related to the very start of the idea of intersectionality. Kimberlé Crenshaw is one of early spokespersons. Crenshaw writes, for example, "Addressing that identity politics actually occurs at the point that classifications are intersecting looks more productive than questioning the idea of thinking about classifications at all."

For example, Crenshaw used the discrimination against females of color as a point of junction of racism and discrimination. As per McCall, the methodology aimed towards a holistic cultural condition. McCall puts her own work in terms of intercategorical intricacy. Her analysis is founded on the deductive approach instead of qualitative techniques, where the other two strategies are descriptive in orientation. Intercategorical ambiguity uses "strategic" terms and may be referred to as "rigorous approach." The analysis of functional relations in several communities is not really about solitary groupings. The normative framework presented depends on the intricacy of relationships between various communities within and throughout empirical findings, and not on intricacies within a solitary cultural circle, a single category, or both. The topic is cross-group, and the approach is routinely contrasted.

With intracategorical or unambiguous intricacy, McCall tends to be accessible to a closer relation between identification and quantification. As she suggests, if sexuality is evaluated, then two groups can be related. If classifications of the working, lower and upper classes are gender-related, there will also be six groups to be analyzed. Two other classes are included with race, and twelve categories are used in comparison. If "Cubans, Mexicans, and Puerto Ricans" had been applied to race, the distinction would have resulted in multi-group experiments of such proportions that the study would have to exclude certain groups "such as sexual identity or race."

Race and class

One of the obstacles that dynamic and even social systems as a whole face is the understanding of race-bound fate. Almost all theorists have concluded that race, not class, has always been the final distinction identifying the important population factors in America, it is evident that class and financial issues are critical for developing a radical agenda and a better society. Why is very little attention paid to why Americans are both resilient to racial issues and are not organized around racial inequality, although they are very capable of recognizing racial problems. The goal is to address the impact of race and class in the creation of a democratic liberal movement.

More pertinently, we dispute that a campaign concentrating on race-neutral issues affecting people in the context of self-interest could build and maintain a national policy of persistent progressiveness. We should prove that it is not possible to develop a radical platform without confronting race. People claiming a race-neutral position typically base their arguments on a very ineffective concept of race and on the work done in carrying out a better social system. This narrow definition of race suggests that it really is mainly about people of color and that bigotry is predominantly about prejudice - and thus an unique appeal. From this perspective, race or racism is mainly understood as a psychosocial event happening among individuals as a bias aimed at non-whites. Disparities can therefore be resolved by recognizing bad, racist offenders and individual perpetrators and by shifting funds between whites and non-whites. The presumption is that this is to be achieved by removing privilege from whites. There is no place in the current paradigm of what we require for a stable, safe life. We therefore view the approach as a zero-sum scenario.

It really isn't shocking that whites are refusing to commit to social engineering. To the extent that class is about hardships, whites are much less likely to become part of the consultation. They claim there is still a wide perception of race, not only about minorities but rather about whites, social structures and cultural concepts that relate to anti-progressive notions. Efforts to establish multiethnic alliances and other unities are weakened by the divisive and restricted use of color.

The narrative of the struggle for nations' rights, equitable organizations and electoral system, and a restricted federal government is drastically unfinished. Similarly, the inequality of urban space in our divided neighborhoods and high-poverty schools cannot easily be addressed merely by state regulation. Both the practices and opposition to reform hinder a radical agenda with adverse implications on whites and non-whites alike. Race is the main reason why the United States, especially to developed nations, is dominated by a nationalist ideology opposed to the notion of supporting those in need.

In the United States, a lot of people believe that race and class are distinguishable or that race can be lessened by class mobility. From this perspective, race differences could be dealt with much more adequately by addressing class. It is both an intellectual and a political position. This series of beliefs are like precepts for many members of the radical white revolution. Are these conclusions false critically, both geographically and practically? Some of the causes are implied in the context in which race is perceived. Yet there are many other explanations for social failure. Class-based solutions are a misleading term and inherently social.

Reform efforts concentrate on moving marginalized people to the level of the middle class instead of changing the interactions between groups to a more equal basis. As a result, we do not have a powerful mobilization tool for creating a strategic coalition on the basis of common values or a sense of unity. Although it is evident that there has to be an emphasis on social and economic problems, whether such an initiative is adequately handled, it is probable that it will not be inclusive or efficient. A democratic solution involves fighting race and creating cross-class, multi-racial alliances. We certainly oppose a decrease in race to class and class to race.

We will demonstrate that race and class, although distinct, are intertwined in the United States, and that ethnic context, culture and experience have influenced and helped define and restrict class awareness. We'll prove the problem is unique in the absence of a labor party, in view of a feeble labor organization. A small, two-tiered social wellbeing program should be the direction toward which we are running. Racialized processes not only have an effect on structural foundations, but also on individual institutions, such as trade unions, with implications for culture as a whole. We also hope to demonstrate how the discriminatory beliefs of whites, the establishment of racial stereotypes and the institutionalization of social structures are related to economic growth and are motivated by public expectations and requirements.

We must question the idea that race is inherently toxic and disrupts the process of creating an alliance with a democratic agenda. It is essentially a statement of tradition and empiricism. Although we can agree that race can and has already been used antagonistically, we suggest that it can also be applied in a positive manner that seeks to draw people together. We intend to illustrate how progressives have been attempting to use color-blind bigotry through rhetorical arguments and coded definitions to dismantle positive initiatives in America. The solution is not to prevent the topic of race, since it is subterranean in the debate. The answer is always race. Even so, we are not saying that we will always be "driving" the race.

The goal here is not to establish a communication technique or an objective basis focused on context, evidential understanding and beliefs.

The racial dimension of class in the United States

Race has made a massive mark, often fully unexplained or overlooked, on American class relations. A deeper examination of the advancement and interaction of race and class in America will reveal the restrictions placed on a race-neutral perspective by radical anti-color coalitions. Our present view of race and class did not come as a consequence of any natural, rational, historical reasoning. Racial and class interpretations have obtained their original meaning and are therefore are not accurate beyond it. They become most meaningful against the background of historical advancement and current race and class interactions.

Since so many of our ethnic views are indicative of our foundational structures and functional modules, this work thinks fondly of a few significant events when these frameworks and myths had been challenged. A detailed description of the interaction between class and race is however far beyond the scope of this report.

Race and class during the New Deal

Class and race are strongly intersecting within the social policy framework that developed during the New Deal. Whereas blacks were often exempt from legal residency by different means, such as poll taxes, they did qualify for certain privileges. The Southern Congress had constitutional veto authority on all civil legislation in its seventeen states and over its thirty four senators. In addition to its impact of the veto, the Southern Democratic Party had been able to create "barriers within the policy proposals of the New Deal and the Reasonable Deal to defend the social structure of its area" by executive positions in main committees, a strong knowledge of parliamentary rules and regulations, and taking advantage of the discrepancy between the strength of their feelings and actual protocols. The early model of the welfare system, built in the mid-1930s, carried the hallmark of Jim Crow colonialism.

The Social Security Act

The Social Security Act has been unsurpassed in American history. It was a guaranteed institution as part of socialist safety programs offering retirement benefits, sustaining family advantages, and offering unemployment insurance and financial support to the poor. Nevertheless, as a result of exemptions for farming and household employees (and other self-employed workers), millions of African Americans were refused protection. Only after Republicans took control over the national government in 1954 were occupational exemptions abolished and initiatives on behalf of the disenfranchised instituted. But many African Americans were never able to make up the 5-year restriction prior to actually collecting welfare.

Help to needy children has been less regional; programs have had flexibility in determining the standard of benefits. Once a state has earned a grant, it regulated public spending. The other key aspect of the Social Security Act was support for the adult needy and the aged. Here, too, the states get to determine the level of benefits. The unemployed compensation system illustrates these approaches. It was less egalitarian when it restricted employees whose employers had already contributed to the plan. In brief, every requirement of old age, social aid, and joblessness under the Social Security Act took on racial contours, and progressive, northern democrats agreed to retain their coalition with the Southern Democrats.

Labor legislation

The National Labor Relations Act (NLRA, 1935) was important as a progressive labor law that sought to promote the needs of the American working class. An exchange of votes was made from the Southerners for the removal of agricultural workers and housekeepers – professional employment groups accessible to African Americans in a racially segregated job market. On occasions where Republicans rejected these rules, the Democratic Party made politically-based changes in order to build a competitive alliance. As a precursor to existing norms, the National Industrial Recovery Act (1933) did not specifically exempt farm and domestic workers. Such exclusions were in fact made summarily by the courts. The new proposals were thus labor-friendly, however uninhabitable they were to the millions of African Americans living far below Mason-Dixon line.

In the 1930s, unionization was rare in the South, but it was significant for the North Democrats, consisting of large labor classes. However, low inflation and growing manufacturing created concerns after the Second World War that such new laws would disrupt the social order of the nation as blacks returned from abroad to the South mobilized labor. Southerners were worried that labor association could intensify civil rights protests and that tight enforcement of the FLSA would lead to pay lowering along ethnic lines. The Southern leaders, who formerly helped create a modern labor system, switched their votes. It was just at this stage that the North Democrats became aligned in resisting the Southern attempts to gain wide-ranging farm exclusions. The subsequent departure of the Southern Democrats from the alliance defending labor rights was disastrous for trade unions, and was especially dangerous for poor blacks.

The result was the Taft-Hartley Act, which significantly restricted the freedom of workers' groups and organizations in general. There are three repercussions relating to social movements: first, the unions pushed to establish concessions where they previously had control. They had not yet been mobilized in the South, and the initiative has failed since Taft-Hartley. In the second half of the twentieth century, unions became equally competent in the Northeast, Midwest, and far west enclaves, with reduced unionization oi the south and on the west coast.

Second, they shifted to concentrate on job problems, such as income, labor laws and standards, and retirement benefits, and therefore restricted the reach of union resources. Third, instead of trying to advocate for social welfare services for those who really need them, they committed to maintaining benefits and health care guarantees and lucrative collective arrangements for their members. That has left unions less class-oriented and less active allies in political coalitions.

Unions have been the only national force ready to express economic problems; so their choices therefore suppressed the momentum of civil rights and needlessly reduced it to non-financial issues. Interestingly, the restricted stance of the unions managed to help soften the issues of race and labor mobility so that the emerging civil rights movement could "shift case law and sculpted constitutional amendment without having skills to remedy economic harm. " Racial divisions yet again restricted the social/financial vision and potential of all Americans.

Immigration, class, and the racial bribe

The Constitution allowed Congress to create a uniform program of naturalization. The Naturalization Act of 1790 provided the very first regulatory description of American nationality. For eighty years, citizen status was restricted to "free white people." Since this first regulatory concept of American nationality was ethnic restricted, the concept of “white” was a subject of huge significance and quantifiable influence. From 1820 to 1860, the United States saw a surge of Irish refugees. The number of Irish-born inhabitants by 1860 was 1.2 million. Fewer immigrants have since come to the United States fully prepared by culture and perspective to interact with African Americans than the Irish, who emerged effectively from their historic conflict and systemic racism in their own land.

In 1842, 70,000 Irish agreed to sign an anti-apartheid address and campaign in Ireland. The famous Irish antislavery proponent, Daniel O'Connell, who headed the huge Irish Independence Repeal movement to break unity with Britain, supported the 1842 initiative. After 1843, there were frequent records that the Irish were strongly opposed to black freedom in America. In reality, the Irish have become the blacks' major opponents. For example, they tried to revive the black mandate in the New York legislature but were defeated in 1826 and 1846 by the initiatives of Tammany Hall Democrats. Between 1830 to 1845, the percentage of the population formed of foreign-born electors increased between one in thirty to one in seven, with the Modern Famine migration generating the largest invasion of foreigners in the antebellum period of American history. Their overwhelming proportions made the ethnic "bribe" feasible and desirable. At the time, Irish whiteness was the focus of much controversy. The Census Bureau held the Irish separate from other classes of the country. A lot of writers and ethnologists mocked the "Celtic Race." For example, George Templeton Strong, a Whig diarist living in New York City, said that the Irish workers in his home had "prehensile paws" instead of hands. Related descriptors used to define the Catholic Irish "race" in the decades before the Civil War.

The Democratic Party aligned itself to gain benefit from the Irish vote. That was achieved by fostering the idea of whiteness, which also broadly included the Scottish, Irish, German, French, and Norman. The Irish modified the manufacturing morality in America and decided to make it all but certain that they would endorse and broaden the policy of white unity promised by the Democratic Party. The conflation of ethnic background with blood might have disturbed the Irish who hated the English, even within the restricted choices and significant costs of antebellum democracy. By driving blacks out of their market segments, they could ignore a language that would become repulsive in the post-revolutionary environment.

The narrative of how the Irish became white regularly occurs in the interpretation of race in America as an important category. The historical background in which only whites could vote and the danger to civil rights presented by natives facilitated an ethnic coercion that would stymie the opportunity for mutual cooperation between classes experiencing the same economic conditions and shared fate. Racial walls hindered the convergence of shared mutual values that would have provided the basis for collective intervention, which, in effect, weakened the economic advancement of working whites in particular along with blacks.

Chapter 7: Police Brutality

Police brutality is the use of increased or needless force by law enforcement in trying to deal with accused persons and innocent citizens. The concept also applies to violations by correctional personnel in city, provincial and national criminal institutions, particularly military prisons.

The term, police brutality, is generally used when directly causing damage to a person. It can entail mental harm thorough bullying techniques used well beyond the legal framework authorized by department policy. From the 18th-20th century, those involved in police violence may have behaved only with the tacit sanction of the municipal judicial system, just like during the Civil Rights Movement. In today's world, people who participate in police misconduct may do so with the implicit consent of their supervisors, or may be corrupt cops. In any case, they will conduct their acts under the letter of the law and, often as not, participate in a corresponding cover up of their unlawful behavior.

In the 2000s, the national government tried to monitor the number of innocent people killed in encounters with the U.S. police, but the initiative was defunded. In 2006, legislation was signed requiring access to police records of killings, but several police forces did not obey these rules. Some reporters and critics issued estimated figures, restricted to the evidence available to them. As per the Washington Post, 1,004 people were killed by the cops in 2019, while 1,098 were murdered by the Mapping Police Violence Project.

Since the 20th century, a number of social, personal, and community-based measures have attempted fight police corruption and violence. These campaigns established a variety of factors that defined police violence, along with the insular structure of the police force (particularly the Blue Wall of Silence), the vigorous defending of police officers, the opposition to reform in police unions, the extensive legislative rights given to police officers (such as constitutional protections), and the systemic bias in police services and the military. The U.S. legal theory of constitutional protections has been highly criticized as "having an almost useless mechanism to encourage police violence to go unprosecuted and deprive suspects their civil rights," as outlined in a 2020 Reuters article.

As far as ideas are concerned, politicians and supporters have taken various approaches. Many who call for police accountability offer concrete proposals for addressing police violence, such as bodycams, civilian advisory commissions, better police discipline, the demilitarization of police departments, and other reforms designed to mitigate abuse (including the Fairness in Policing Act of 2020). Many support the de-funding of police departments in favor of a completely or partial reallocation of funds for civic and social welfare. Those supporting police reform have asked for the police to be disbanded and reconstructed from the bottom up. Many who endorse the abolition of police services request police departments to be completely abolished and substituted by other cultural and social providers.

Police killings in registered U.S. cases

Case 1: Eric Garner

Eric Garner was murdered on July 17, 2014 on Staten Island, New York (Harkinson, 2014). Eric Garner was a black male, 43, who had been assaulted by police officers in New York City for selling non- taxable cigarettes. Garner was an asthmatic father of six murdered by police officer, Daniel Pantaleo, using a chokehold. The justice department decided not to bring a perjury case against Pantaleo. The very last phrases from Garner were, "I can't even breathe!" Putting one in a chokehold is a practice prohibited by in 1993.

Case 2: John Crawford

John Crawford, a 22-year-old black man, was shot dead by a cop on August 5, 2014 in Beavercreek, Ohio at Walmart. A 911 phone call was made about a man pointing a gun in a Walmart store (Harkinson, 2014). The gun to which they alluded was Crawford's, a s177 caliber BB rifle allegedly taken from the retail store. The footage uploaded of Crawford's shooting disproved the police's story about what happened. The police said they shot Crawford after continually asking him to drop the rifle. Nevertheless, the video reveals that Crawford was fired soon after speaking with the police (Balko, 2015). The footage also shows that Crawford did not aim the gun at anybody, which really is radically different from what an observer said to the 911 dispatcher. An eyewitness reported that Crawford had pointed his rifle at him, and the eyewitness even reiterated this assertion to the press (Balko, 2015). After seeing the security footage, the eyewitness altered his statement. LeeCee Johnson, Crawford 's girlfriend, was on Crawford 's cellphone when he was killed. LeeCee clarified that Crawford had told her he had been in Walmart's toy department, that carried toy guns. She claimed, "It's not true" but the police began firing (Balko, 2015). The police ordered Crawford to get down after he had already been fired on. There was no effort to contra-escalate the circumstances on the part of the police.

Case 3: Samuel DuBose

At Cincinnati University, Officer, Ray Tensing, fatally fired and murdered Sam DuBose, an innocent weaponless black man during a routine traffic stop. Tensing decided to stop DuBose for a missing front plate number (Blow, 2015). Apparently, Tensing had lost his patience because DuBose would not get out of the vehicle and was quick extract his rifle and fire on DuBose in the neck (London and Hagrman, 2015). DuBose 's parents said that DuBose had health issues. Because of his health problems, he might have not been strong enough to confront the officer or escape the vehicle easily (London and Hagrman, 2015).

As per the examination of the DuBose police shooting, "Tensing had been passed by a Honda Accord car owner and was allowed to kill the driver with his service pistol" (Blow, 2015). He also reported that he just fired a single shot and was impelled by a truck to pull his gun. Even so, the story proves that every one of his statements was incorrect. The body camera footage played a vital part in the trial in Sam DuBose, focused on the misleading views expressed by Officer Tensing.

The prosecutor clarified that DuBose chose not to take direct measures against Officer Tensing. He explained that Officer Tensing had not been pulled to the ground, but had dropped back after DuBose had been fired in the neck region. He also remarked on Tensing's attempt to confuse interrogators. DuBose's family lawyer, named O'Mara, mentioned how rapidly the incident had taken place. Upon seeing the footage, O'Mara said she was waiting to see all of the unfolding incident and was shocked at how easily the shooting occurred and that the car pulled away instantly.

Case 4: Laquan McDonald

Laquan McDonald, a 17-year-old black man, was murdered by Chicago policeman, Jason Van Dyke, on October 20, 2014. Van Dyke had a background of criticism throughout his tenure as a police officer (Fantz, 2015). The allegations spoke mainly about the use of unnecessary force and Van Dyke had even been suspected of using a racial insult (Fantz, 2015). In the overwhelming majority of suspicious cases, Van Dyke was resolved. Due his use of unreasonable force on the day of the traffic violation, the judge fined the Chicago officer $350,000. Van Dyke's past actions seems to indicate an attempt to assassinate Laquan. Laquan was fired at 16 times. There was no excuse for one policeman to shoot 16 times at another person, particularly someone who did not represent a danger to Van Dyke 's life. Video clearly showed that Laquan was heading down sidewalk, away from several policemen. The police later confirmed that McDonald was holding a metal four-inch knife. Van Dyke was the first officer to shoot his weapon along with at least eight other cops. Even so, McDonald's back seemed to be in the direction of the cop cars while he was fired upon. Policeman Van Dyke, "the very first policeman to be prosecuted with first-degree assassination since 1980," was convicted of second-degree murder. Van Dyke was convicted on sixteen allegations of agitated firearm battery, one per shot being fired at McDonald.

Case 5: Tamir Rice

Tamir Rice was a twelve-year-old boy whose life was ended in seconds due to police brutality. An agreement had been made with Tamir's parents and the City of Cleveland, where even the City had to pay $6 million to Tamir's parents in response to the state lawsuit they filed (Pearson, 2016). The conditions of the settlement did not, however, criticize the city. Preceding Tamir's murder, a 911 caller said that the boy was in the local park holding what seemed to be a toy rifle. Officer Timothy Loehman, a staff member, fatally shot and killed Tamir after the phone call had been made. The special prosecutor was unable to prosecute Officer Loehmann or his mentor, Officer Frank Garmback. The special prosecutor found that the killing of Tamir was not a criminal offense, but instead a "natural consequence of general human mistake, error and interaction."

The defamation lawsuit by Tamir 's parents asserted that the city showed carelessness and that the emergency responders might have described to the policemen that Tamir probably had a toy rifle. Tamir's parents said that "the officers entered the scenario too violently and Loehmann fired too soon, failing to protect the young man when he was killed" (Pearson, 2016). In this regard, Tamir's parents also claimed that Loehmann was ill-advised to be a policeman but that there was a failure by the metro area to correctly direct its policemen. The city reacted by putting the blame on Tamir instead of the government. The City argued that they were obligated to protection regarding federal statutes (Pearson, 2016).

Case 6: Sandra Bland

Because most police brutality incidents usually involve young black men, young black girls are suffer from violent police acts. Sandra Bland's life had been seized by law enforcement authorities. She was apprehended during a traffic violation, assaulted by the cops and then jailed (Stanford, 2015). During her detention, Bland screamed for the policeman to quit punching her, and that the policeman was breaking her ribs. Bland was found murdered in jail in Waller County Texas. In Texas, the jury judge did not prosecute any of the police for Bland 's murder, namely Trooper Encinia, who first hauled Bland off after her pursuit.

Case 7: Freddie Gray

In Baltimore, Freddie Gray died of police brutality on April 19, 2015. Gray was a twenty-five-year-old African American man who also suffered spinal cord injuries when he was apprehended. The mayor of Baltimore, Stephanie Rawlings Blake, has pushed tirelessly to grant the police chief the authority to punish policemen. Since last year, Baltimore has registered one hundred and seven homicides. Baltimore authorities agree that the most successful way to avoid police brutality is by learning. Police Chief Anthony Batts has recommended that officers wear video body cameras. Batts also agreed to bargain with the police association in order to be able to effectively discipline policemen for their actions of police brutality.

Case 8: Steve Eugene Washington

In 2010, the judge granted nearly $four million to two Los Angeles police officers, George Diego and Allan Corrales, who fatally fired Steve Eugene Washington, a twenty-seven-year-old autism spectrum disorder black man (Hanson, 2015). As per the case, that was an incident of retaliatory prejudice. The policemen attempted to claim that Steve had given them a "black stare" that the police officers deemed suspicious (Hanson, 2015). Steve grabbed his waistband to snatch his mobile and was fired in the back. The only penalty for this against law killing was for the policemen to be susceptible to obligation.

Case 9: Stephon Clarke

Stephon Clarke was fired and assassinated by Sacramento policemen on March 18, 2018 at his grandmother's house (Levenson et al, 2018). The deadly shot was captured on the policeman's body camera and a police helicopter. Policemen replied to a call alleging that a person had smashed vehicle windows and had been hidden in a courtyard. Policemen rushed to the front yard, following Stephon. The policemen claimed that Stephon was holding what looked to be a firearm. The policemen then shot at him twenty times, and he was beaten numerous times. Stephon was defenseless and the entity in Stephon's hand referred to by the policemen was Stephon's mobile phone (Levenson et al, 2018). The officers accountable for the killing of Stephon Clarke went back to work. Cops told ABC news that the identities of the guilty officers involved had not been release and they had no plans to publish their identities.

After the recent killing of George Floyd, everyone's feeds have been crowded with images of police brutality. You can't get out of your mind those shaky, candid images of white cop, Derek Chauvin with his knee on Floyd 's neck for about nine minutes, smothering him to death in full daylight. Such brutality has led to protests and mental devastation. We are now constantly subjected to pictures of unarmed civilians who have been stabbed, shot and gassed by a corrupt police force. Protests have not only unfolded in the U.S., but also in every nation around the world. Police brutality has not been accepted by global protesters who are fighting this war as their own.

It is similar to what was described above in regard to the United Kingdom, where police impose violence on black men four times more often than their white peers, though black people actually make up 3.3 percent. In fact, they make up twelve percent of law enforcement confrontations using force. Cases such as Sarah Reed, who died in Holloway Prison, London, became the center of a violent police scenario in 2012. Police officer, James Kiddie, pulled her by the hair, tossed her on the ground, squeezed her neck, and repeatedly kicked her in the head. The incident also involves Julian Cole, who had been hanged by six law enforcement officers at a nightclub in 2013. His leg was fractured but Julian was not kill, but the path of his life was completely altered after such police brutality.

Once it has been revealed as overt deaths at the hands of the police, black men seem more likely to be killed in police custody under critical condition than white people. Across races, there've been four hundred and two deaths and no arrests in state custody since 1990 in the UK. In 2011, mass protests and instability were seen all over London following the attack of Mark Duggan – a killing in prison. The real story will never ever be properly understood. The press wrongly claimed that Duggan started the violence with a shot and they were bent on depicting him as a mob boss. Stafford Scott, primarily assigned as the Operation Trident Advisor, stepped down from the police staff after complaints, as reported in The Guardian. “[GIEC's] inquiry is inaccurate and is likely to be sullied – mostly because we can never have belief in its latest presentation.” Two other members of the general public stepped down from the inquiry, one willing to call the body 's research "shoddy "and another reacting to its official draft.

The policemen were not equipped, really just a half-truth. The police carry stun guns that are more than four times as likely to be used on people of black color. They have also been implicated in killings such as that of Dalian Atkinson in 2016.

Then there are the situations that take place behind the closed doors of the penal system about which there will never be full clarification or accountability. In jails, abuse in the form of neglect of prisoner’s health serve as a means of indirect aggression. Sarah Reed's subsequent death in jail in 2016 reveals the horrific effects of ignoring an inmate’s mental health issues. Reed had severe, long-standing psychological problems and was found murdered in her cell; allegedly she did not obtain the medicine she needed. In 2017, Anabella Landsberg was stabbed to death in her HMP Peterborough jail bed. Force had been used. In the hours after her death, a doctor poured a glass of chilled water on her corpse, which still lay on the ground and reported that Landsberg was "getting treatment and falsifying her medical problems." Landsberg was insulin dependent.

Around twenty years since the Stephen Lawrence investigation, the conclusions of the study have remained true: United Kingdom police are systemically biased. The explanations given are not exhaustive – they will never be – but they demonstrate how the police system is overwhelmingly abusive of black citizens.

Black people are more than 8 times more probably to be stopped and investigated by the police around the world

Many from BAME (black, Asian, minority and ethnic) communities are unfairly affected by the growing “actually stopped-and-search” control of the police all over the world. In London, blacks seem to be even more than nine times more likely to be the victim of this tactic, while not guilty of any crimes. Police are accused of “conventioning” and “victimizing” BAME people by virtue of the powers conferred on them by Section sixty of the Criminal Justice and Public Order Act. All in all, many from BAME heritage are four times more likely to be halted under provocative criterion compared to white people.

The metropolitan police in London are four times more likely to use strength against blacks

Statistics from the 2017-2018 era found that the Metropolitan police in London were four times more likely to use violence towards blacks than whites as a percentage of the total population. Publicly accused of "stereotyping" black youths in England, a white police officer was labeled racist after handcuffing a black person who was considered to be an aid worker near his home in London. A search yielded no result, however and he wasn't arrested.

Black people in London are significantly two times more likely to be charged for pandemic lockdown offences

In the wake of the coronavirus outbreak that affects BAME overwhelmingly, the metropolitan police are significantly more likely to punish blacks with coronavirus infections versus white people. Blacks, who make up twelve percent of the London's population also make up a third of the prosecutions for suspected infringements of the shut-down rule. Asians in London are twenty-six percent more likely to be charged by the cops, while whites are twenty-three percent less likely to be prosecuted.

BAME individuals are two time as likely to die after prudence has already been used

Charity survey statistics on deaths in detention where confinement is a characteristic indicate that BAME people seem more than two times as likely to die than most other homicides. They are much more likely to suffer from the use of power and incur almost double the killings over mental health problems.

Although the British police are not regularly equipped with them, the use of neck chains are legally permitted for use by London policemen. In the summer of 2017, four black youths were killed in the city after being held back by the police. In one instance, a spectators claimed that the cop had knelt on the man's back for '8 to 10 minutes,' while the crowd pled to them to leave, similar to what is seen in the footage of the killing of George Floyd in a chokehold.

Chapter 8: Cultural Appropriation

Cultural appropriation, sometimes referred to as cultural embezzlement, is the inclusion of a component or aspects of other culture in a different context. This can be problematic as representatives of a mainstream society rarely come from marginalized minority communities.

As per its critics, cultural appropriation varies from acculturation, forced integration or equitable cultural diversity; however it is a kind of colonialism. When cultural features are borrowed from a marginalized culture by representatives of a majority community, they are incorporated without their initial historical environment – and even sometimes despite the explicit approval of representatives of the initiating community.

Cultural exploitation is directly opposed to some communities and persons, along with the native population who campaign for cultural protection and those who fight for universal intellectual property laws of heritage, immigrant cultures and may have suffered or remain under colonialism. Sometimes it is inevitable when different cultures come together that cultural appropriation may contain the misuse of another culture's spiritual practices, fashion, views, or literature and music.

Some who find such theft to be oppressive say that the initial significance of the appropriated cultural relics is destroyed or altered when they are separated from their initial cultural sources and that they are insensitive or even a form of profanity. Cultural features that may have a significant meaning in a given cultural identity may be seen as an "unusual" style by the larger majority. Kjerstin Johnson wrote that as appropriation is accomplished, the imitator who, "does not undergo that oppression is capable of 'playing' for a short time 'exotic,' without undergoing any of the regular discriminations experienced by other cultures."

The definition of ethnic theft has been widely questioned. Observers assert that the term is sometimes confusing or misused by the normal community, and that allegations of "racial appropriation" are often misinterpreted in circumstances, including when consuming meals from a range of cultures or even hearing about other cultures. Others claim that the practice of cultural appropriation as generally described does not substantially represent social damage or that the word lacks philosophical coherence. Yet others contend that the word imposes artificial limitations on artistic freedom, artists' self-expression, collective distinctions, or their own sense of enmity or resentment rather than emancipation.

Overview

Cultural appropriation may constitute the use of concepts, inscriptions, artifacts, or other elements of human-made linguistic or non-linguistic culture. As a term contentious in interpretation, the possession of cultural theft has always been the topic of much discussion. Adversaries of cultural appropriation regard numerous examples as improper utilization when the particular originating culture is a marginalized culture or is subservient to the dominant culture in social, political, financial or conventional warfare, or when other concerns are engaged, including the ethnic or religious confrontation.

Linda Martín Alcoff argues that this is also found in cultural invaders' usage of the representations of a marginalized society or other cultural aspects thereof, including music, dance, ceremonial rituals, clothing, expression, and social conduct, where these components are cheapened and used for advertising instead of valued in their actual cultural context (such as Kim Kardashian's Kimono clothing line). Adversaries find problems of colonization. The history and distinction between exploitation and reciprocal trade are important to the study of cultural appropriation. Many claim that reciprocal sharing takes place in a "fair playing field," because theft means aspects of an exploited community being extracted out of proportion from those marginalized by those who lack the cultural background to better appreciate, accept, or use such components.

Another separate interpretation of cultural appropriation argues that the criticism of cultural appropriation is "a profoundly conservative initiative," given its revolutionary origins and "first attempts to maintain the substance of an existing community in formaldehyde and secondly attempts to discourage anyone from engaging with that culture." Proponents' interpretation is either innocuous or mutually advantageous, citing anomalies and brand diversion.

Academic study

Cultural appropriation is a fairly recent component of scholarly research. The word originated in the 1980s in the form of a pre-independence critique of Western imperialism, such as Kenneth Coutts-Smith's "Few Specific findings on the Problems of Cultural Colonialism" written in 1976.

Cultural and ethnic theorist, George Lipsitz, used the words "tactical pro-essentialism" to apply to the deliberate use of a cultural type, beyond one's own, to describe oneself or one's community. Strategic anti-essentialism can be found across both minority groups and dominant cultures and is not limited to the use of the other. However, Lipsitz suggests that as the dominant society tries to politically anti-essentialism itself by appropriating a minority culture, it must take particular care to consider the unique socio-historical context and meaning of cultural structures so as not to reinforce the already current majority vs. minority hierarchical power dynamics. This covers different elements, such as:

- Art, literature, iconography, and adornment
- Religion and spirituality
- Fashion

Urban music and style

In order to get a deeper comprehension of youth hip hop music culture and gangster rap, it is necessary to talk about its artistic as well as visual context. To appreciate today's popular music, you need to consider its wider context, including the past and aspirations of young black people. Modern black rap music and entertainment are linked to traditional African folk history and tradition (Rabaka, 2012). Rabaka (2012) reveals that rap music as well as other aspects of hip hop culture, such as reggae ton, rock rap, metal rap, tour hop and so forth are based on the famous black music and culture of past generations. The origins of the lyrics can be identified in traditional blues, ragtime, jazz, gospel, rock and drum and bass music (Rabaka, 2012 & Robinson, 1999). The above-mentioned genres are drenched with "so many flourishing beats that seem to contain schizophrenic mean-mugging rhetoric, like 'homosexual-hating', 'bitch-beating,' 'pimp-slapping,' and 'ho-smacking," (Rabaka, 2012: p2) that can be found in rap and youth music culture (Rabaka, 2012).

Throughout the description above is the historical context of hip hop culture and gangster rap found in the aspirations of the Bronx community. In this section, we seek to understand the early history of music. Besides, rap music represents more than just the emotions of poor black youth and affluent white teenagers (Rabaka, 2012). It all began with classical African music, which tried to give the directors the chance to express their personal thoughts. Thus,, they have been able to turn human interactions into common music and a unique social language. The themes of these songs are very plain, but also packed with strong feelings, aboriginal phrases, metaphors, folk philosophy, and spiritual manners. Traditional African music influenced initial African American songs, with the addition of parables, double sounds, and allusions that emerged from the hardships of African American individuals during enslavement and the restoration period - i.e. pre-reconstruction, and colonization (Rabaka, 2012).

African American music culture was one of the several items permitted during the slavery era in the United States. The African people were under tyranny; the Americans demolished nearly all that belongs to African culture, including literature, religious beliefs, and personal values. Music was something they were permitted to retain even when they celebrated Christian events and performed for their white masters. A few of the vestiges of African rhythms have been conserved, and some of the original black ethnic heritage was kept below slavery. This may be attributed to the days of the injustice of slavery and African American pop culture, which included music but has however come to mean the African American community where black traditions had to be protected (Wall, 2003). Modern African American music became the cornerstone of blues in the late 19th century. The blues evolved into a diverse artistic musical and cultural genre with a significant expressive dimension that varied, depending on the performer with the location, the crowd, and the context (Rabaka, 2012).

Rabaka (2012) strives to make blues the initial form of "black mainstream music" and "black mainstream culture." Modern music culture, rock music and rap are deeply embedded in the blues' aesthetic. Blues and gangsta rap are about the same, in that blues music and the blues cultural heritage defined black Americans at the end of the 20th century, while gangster rap and popular music defined African Americans at the turn of the 21st century. The significant change in blues culture and popular music can be seen in the advancements made in female issues, gender equality, human liberties, and information technology in the 20th century.

Reformation and increased awareness enlightened the discussion of hip hop. Blues became the foundation of the history of rhythm and blues hip hop; however, the effect was not particularly strong. Blues motivates the emotional content of the Black Movement in jazz. Orchestration features syncopated rhythms, melodic complexity, and elements of swing, all focusing on equipment instead of song choices. Thus, certain facets of jazz are not motivated by blues or even African American music. Jazz consists of various components, revealing a new diorama of this enduring genre, which includes folk music, blues, field hollers, ragtime, parades, and western Europe orchestral music (Rabaka, 2012).

Rap music and hip hop culture were part of Rabaka's literature, with repercussions for philosophy, history, society, and aesthetics (2012). Rap and hip hop embody the rage-filled emotions of African Americans during the civil liberties revolution as well as the Black Power struggle, and the women's movement. The genre of music of the civil rights, recognized as R&B, spilled over into the rock culture of the era. R&B was influenced by jazz and went on to contribute to folk music of the civil rights movement. Folk music, jazz and disco formed the context of the Black Women's Liberation struggle. Such music ultimately contributed to the rap and neo-folk music of the rock revival (Rabaka, 2012). Rabaka suggests that gangster rap and popular music reflect vibrant hope and dark pessimism, countercultural tragedy, and the spiritual triumphs that mark the era of civil rights, Black Power, and Women 's Liberation.

Chapter 9: Biases Conscious or Unconscious

A bias is a habit, propensity, or prejudice against something or someone. Many prejudices are constructive— like preferring to consume only foods deemed safe or keeping away from someone who has knowingly done harm. Yet prejudices also focus on assumptions, rather actual persons or institutional awareness. Cognitive shortcuts, positive or negative, can lead to prejudices that lead to rash decisions or illegal acts.

In the literature, two forms of bias have been established.

Conscious

In this type of bias, the participant is very clear about his / her perceptions and emotions when it comes to tacit or conscious actions performed with intent. Cognitively, this form of bias is characterized by overt negative actions conveyed by physical and verbal violence or through more direct means such as omission of reason. Perpetrators are often guilty of politically incorrect acts.

Implicit or unconscious

Implicit or implicit bias occurs beyond the consciousness of the individual and can be in direct contradiction with personal convictions and values inherited as a child. What is so problematic about racial bias is that it inevitably falls outside a person's full consciousness.

If you are hiring based on "good feeling," you are probably hiring based on unconscious prejudice. The effective way to avoid capitulating to racist attitudes is to become aware of them and take action when recruiting, hiring, and retaining employees to prevent bias. That will help your team enjoy a more diverse and therefore productive work environment.

How bias affects decision-making

“Many of us assume to be legal and impartial. We assume we are good decision-makers, able to size up a job applicant or a business deal objectively by reach a reasonable and rational conclusion that is in our national or organization’s interest. According to Harvard University researcher, Mahzarin Banaji, in the Harvard Business Review. "More than two decades of studies indicate that in fact most of us are dreadfully short of our inflated view of ourselves."

Conscious and implicit prejudice profoundly affects our choices and views. In other words, our perceptions and responses towards others. This can influence how open or polite we are toward other people (i.e. whether we are "on guard"), the things we perceive or label as most relevant in communicating with others, and even our listening skills. If we harbor an implicit bias, we may not be actively listening to what the individual says, as we have already made the judgment that they are not worth talking to. If we recruit someone for a job, make friends at our workplace or try to promote someone, prejudice affects virtually every decision in front of us. Our biased decisions stop some people from acceding to the same life and career prospects as others. It eventually costs companies billions per year in revenues.

The cost of bias

While prejudice has many detrimental effects on its victims, it also has negative impacts on organizations that are unable to retain leading talent. Biased entities lack creativity and build a bad reputation by not having a diverse workforce. Attributing the losses of a company to implicit bias, or assessing the impact of intentional bias is often difficult. Diversity consultant, Paul Skovron, suggests that we investigate the cost of racism and the resulting arbitrations.

Prejudice, which is closely linked to conscious bias, can help us identify the economic impact of bias on companies. According to research by Involve and CEBR 2018, every year the UK economy loses out on a total of £ 127 billion due to discrimination. Broken down, £123bn derived from discrimination based on gender, with £2.6 from discriminatory practices against BAME people. Different racial employees are said to earn £ 152 more per week on average compared to their white colleagues; white employees earn £ 67-209 more per week than their black or brown colleagues. Removing discrimination in terms of gender and ethnic background would not only favor most individuals and employers, but it would also improve the overall environment. Experts estimate that an egalitarian workforce could raise UK GDP by 7 percent.

How do microaggressions actually harm people?

Evidence demonstrates that microaggressions, while clearly minor and often harmless crimes, can take a significant psychological toll on their recipients' mental health. It can lead to frustration and depression, which is likely to impair productivity at work and problem-solving capabilities.

Microaggressions can even cause physical health problems

They may influence a work or school environment, making it more confrontational while perpetuating dangerous stereotyping. Stereotyping stems from the fear of confirming existing stereotypes about one's community, which can have a negative effect on trust and achievement.

None of this is hard to fathom if you consider how microaggressions could affect your life if you were subjected to a continuous flow of insults and cruelties. Think about how it would feel to always have to brace for or recover from an offence. It's not just about getting upset: some researchers have found that microaggressions can even cause physical ailments.

Are microaggressions the same as racism, sexism, and homophobia?

They are premised on many of the same core ideas about minorities or those groups that have been stigmatized in America (for example, people deemed not intelligent, those that they don't relate normally, or that make for mockery). But microaggressions are distinct from overtly racist, sexism, or homophobic acts or comments, even though they usually have no malicious intent or hatred behind them.

In a series of YouTube videos on the subject, the author, Dr. Derald Wing Sue, explained, "People who engage in cultural appropriation are ordinary people who experience themselves as good, moral, decent individuals. Microaggressions occur because they are outside the victim's level of conscious awareness."

"It's (is not) the blatant racists, the white nationalists, the gang, the skinheads." However, "that makes them all the more threatening in certain respects." The pure bigots, "are less likely to influence my quality of living than well-intentioned people — educators, employers, healthcare professionals — who are ignorant of their prejudices."

In this manner, stereotypes are strongly related to unconscious prejudices, which are the behaviors, perceptions, and perceptions we ignore, which can sneak into our minds and influence our behavior (also known as "think about people you didn't know you had"). A person with racial prejudice toward blacks may have difficulty linking the term "black" with positive terms on the Implicit Association Test, a computerized test designed to determine how closely we associate certain topics. Therefore, think of microaggressions as less manifestations of overt racism, deliberate bigoted remarks than unconscious prejudices that come into our lives in our everyday interactions. And yes, we all have different biases at some stage and are likely to be exposed to a microaggression.

Are people who complain about microaggressions too sensitive?

There's strong animosity in some camps against the notion that a "innocent" comment could be considered problematic. Referring to that same video on YouTube, Dr. Sue says:

"I have to say that analyzing segments and sub-aggression is annoying to me. Our society is a society of over-sensitive people. What occurred to be smart enough to know that people will react and sometimes do things that are incompetent. The earlier we avoid wasting time pointing out normal human behaviors, the sooner we can bring the time into stronger, more efficient fields of study."

"The theory of [microaggression] typically characterizes people of color as poor and helpless, and promotes a culture of victimization rather than an opportunity society."

Such a critique appears to fit into the wider debate regarding multiculturalism and "political correctness" in which resistance frequently contains an implicit doubt about the seriousness of oppressed people's arguments. There is a sense that it is too much trouble or is impossible to avoid actions that trigger damage.

Stop for and think before you speak, especially when weighing in on someone's identity

It's not very difficult to put some thought into the prejudices you might have, become intrigued about how others interpret your statements and deeds, listen when people explain why some statements offend them, and make it a habit to stop and think before you speak, especially when weighing in on someone's heritage. Be very cautious about your own prejudices and fears. Seek to interact with various people in terms of race, culture, ethnicity, and other qualities. Be open to sharing your overt or implicit prejudices and how they might affect others. Be an ally, instead, fighting against all types of racism and prejudice on a personal level.

Chapter 10: Racism: Personal and Institutional

Institutional racism often is referred to as structural racism, a type of racism demonstrated in the context of societal organizations. This contributes to inequality in the fields of criminal law, jobs, housing, health and well-being, democratic power and education, amongst other concerns.

Individual racism is the behavior of those who promote or maintain insidious bigotry. Individual racism take place mostly on a barely conscious level with some degree of cognitive awareness. It can be voluntary or involuntary.

Take a look at individual racism at the point of the subconscious. A white guy who locks his car door when an African American steps by, the unwillingness to talk to an Asian man, the rejection of meeting a black woman based on race not mentality. Other examples include not wanting to employ a Latino thinking he would be unmotivated. All this reflects stereotyping. Personal racism is a cognitive awareness and is recognized as a type of discrimination.

A Discussion of individual, institutional, and cultural racism

As HRD (Human Resource Development) study, practice, and discourse on diversity continue to expand, the literature addressing inequality in the U.S. in a systemic manner is scanty. For example, the questions mostly raised in every human mind include: 1) Why is multicultural awareness and training required in organizations and the current culture? 2) What precisely does prejudice mean? 3) Does racism directly impact individuals and organizations and in what way? 4) In what respects will prejudice impact individuals and organizations going forward?

Human Resource Development (HRD) is a structure or framework to assist workers in improving their personal and corporate capacities, experience, and skills. HRD is one of the most essential incentives that workers pursue when perceived as an employee. Continuing to improve their talents, with support, assists in attracting and inspiring workers.

We want to revisit the wider social concept of racism and discrimination in the U.S. We have to understand it from a historical and current perspective, to elucidate social racism. The methodological and analytical perspective of Critical Race Theory – CRT (Bell, 1993) is instructive in this regard. It is proposed as a structure that offers contextual comprehension for academics, professionals and interested parties, searching for current ways to address ethnicity, colonialism, and culture questions. CRT methodology builds a groundwork for moving beyond the activist civil rights era towards an inclusiveness and acceptance in U.S. society. Finally, we need to address implications for HRD research, and practice to involve the HRD field in the formulation of guidelines to demolish persistent acts of personal, cultural and technological racism right now.

Methodology

In choosing an effective research approach to address racism at the human, systemic, and social level, we undertook an analysis of the literature on the different types of racism and reviewed a selection of studies from a variety of fields to discuss the current situation in the United States regarding historical and current racism.

We elected to shape the investigation as a statistical view of racism, focusing mainly on research-based proof that endorses its historical and current effects on people, organizations, and traditions.

Review of the literature on racism in the United States

We propose a current and historical analysis of the key literature relating to HRD academicians and researchers on racism. There has been a broad range of information: 1) a U.S. definition of racism, 2) U.S. individual racism, 3) U.S. institutional racism and 4) U.S. traditional racism. Racism in the U.S. is to be described and reconsidered.

The purpose of this undertaking is to distinguish the term, racism, from the term, discrimination, in order to lay the foundation for further discussion. Due to its use in the National Advisory Commission Report on Civil Disorders (1968), the term, racism, has become popular. Racism has become a frequent subject of inquiry in African American studies (West, 1993), cognitive science (Klinker & Smith, 1999), and philosophy (Feagin & Vera, 1995). It also has a wider scope of concentration on organizations as well as individuals within the culture (Ladson-Billings, 1995), psychology (Freud, 1924), There is more international awareness (Banks, 1981a, 1981b) and management knowledge on multiculturalism (Cox, 1993; Thomas, 1991). Countless problems have explored by scholarly disciplines that offer progressive solutions to promoting racial equity. They explore the tension between the principles of inclusion and the school of segregation that attempts to legitimize inequality through discrimination (i.e., color dumb) laws and race-conscious district boundaries, to list but a few (Bell, 1993).

Racism often has to do with bigotry and stereotyping but in a systemic way. Discrimination, racism, and stereotyping allude to unequal societal practices, perceptions, and values. Discrimination may be elaborated as an unreasonable, destructive emotion towards members of a target population that includes disputing the "fair and equitable treatment for groups of individuals they might well desire." Prejudice is generally described as an unjust and nasty mindset towards a social category or perceived individuals belonging to that community. A stereotypical assumption is a general statement of opinion regarding a group or its leaders that is irrational because it represents flawed thought mechanisms or overgeneralization, empirical inconsistency, unreasonable rigidity, an incorrect trend, or the justification of a prejudiced mindset or anti-racist conduct.

On the other hand, racism may be seen as the organized interaction between specific types of assumptions, prejudices, and discrimination. Studies suggest three main racist concepts. First, prejudice is embedded in assumptions about basic biological and social distinctions (stereotypes). Second, discrimination includes differentiated biased judgments and emotions towards a different community (prejudice) relative to one's own. Either the other community is expressly defined as weaker, or it is assumed that one's own community is superior. Third, prejudice represents in individuals and organizations the unequal treatment of populations (discrimination) in ways that continue to reinforce biased views, behaviors, and outcomes.

Racism, in fact, entails not only prejudiced views and opinions, but also the social forces that foster unequal consequences that favor other races or exist at the detriment of others by giving one's own race special advantages. As stated by Feagin and Vera (1995), "Racism is much more than a matter of human bigotry, and scattered incidents of discrimination." This reflects the existence of a generally-recognized discriminatory philosophy and the right to withhold from certain ethnic classes the "dignity, privileges, rights, and benefits" offered to one's own race through "a collectively structured collection of beliefs, behaviors, and activities." Whereas psychologists have traditionally examined intrapsychic (e.g., perceptual, behavioral, or psychodynamic) mechanisms and relationships between people in terms of prejudices, bigotry, and inequality, racism exists on a much wider social stage. Jones (1997) describes two social-level manifestations of prejudice. The first is social bigotry, which refers to the collective action of personal perceptions, biases, and inequality in order to build and encourage differences within members of communities. The second is institutional racism that relates to conscious or unconscious exploitation or acceptance of institutional policies (for example, poll taxes, admission requirements) that disproportionately limit the rights of specific sections of the population.

Institutional racism in the United States defined and revisited

Institutional racism includes the distinct impact of policies, practices, and legislation on representatives of certain ethnic groups and on organizations as a whole. Institutional bias emerges from deliberate prejudice (e.g., by controlling immigration based on stereotypes), offering preferential support to one's personal group (e.g., efforts to restrict the voting rights of another community), or as a side-product of policies of a specific objective stemming from systemic race-based policies that are usually interconnected. Of note, Caucasian Americans have established racial ideologies that are intended to validate laws that accomplish two significant types of economic oppression: slavery and the confiscation of land from local tribes (Klinker & Smith, 1999).

While the assumption that race is a biological concept is central to racism, racism is in reality a social structure that encourages one party to manipulate another through the creation of an agenda that supports this behavior (Fields, 1990). As per Fields, although individual populations are racialized (e.g. Africans, African Americans, Italians, Jews), one must consider the role of the majority culture. For example, the slavery of African Americans in the United States for centuries had been a response to the need for cheap labor on farmlands. In the beginning of the 1900s, during the substantial migration from southern Europe, Italians were described as racially and morally inferior. In Nazi Germany, Jews were insidiously racialized for state financial and social benefit.

In addition, Fields concluded that while individual racism may contribute to public support for legislation that results in structural or systematic racism. It may be free of individual racism and includes the active participation of persons with a commitment to segregation. Institutional bias is often "ritualized" in ways that diminish the commitment and resources of the people and communities desiring to fight it (Feagin & Vera, 1995). Nevertheless, as soon as such laws and regulations are developed, individual or group action, based on expectations and the knowledge of unjust outcomes, become critical to counter them (Cox, 1993; Thomas, 1991).

Generally, structural prejudice is not regarded as culturally discriminatory, since it is expressed in legislation (usually believed to be good and moral), is ritualistic, and is followed by racist narratives (Feagin & Vera, 1995). Nevertheless, as per Feagin and Vera, what is observed as equitable can vary from one point of view to another. One such viewpoint is micro-justice (Fields, 1990) that incorporates conceptions of justice applicable to particular people and reflects how interactions among people are equal (e.g. procedural justice). Another viewpoint is macro-justice (Fields, 1990) that relates to the concept of equity that incorporates a wider social, economic, legal and ethical arena and examines whether results over time are equal (distributive justice). Policies and regulations that tend to be equitable at the micro level may well be discriminatory at a more systemic level (Cox, 1993; Thomas, 1991).

Cox (1993) argued that even though institutional racism is not generally deliberate or expressly established, its procedure is often deduced from divergent consequences among racial groups empirically attributed to unreasonable policy, even that seemingly anti-race-related. As per Jones (1997), the consequences occur socially (e.g. in loan policies), in the employment environment (e.g. recruitment and wage inequalities and ethnic and sexual misconduct), in school (e.g. enrollment and welfare support initiatives), in the media (e.g. excessive-representation of communities identified with crime or poverty), and in the criminal justice process (e.g. racial or gender bias). Jones additionally argued that racist beliefs and ideals are still profoundly rooted in the fabric of civilization such that they tend to determine what is natural and acceptable for society generally, a trend known as cultural racism.

Theoretical framework

While this discussion has presented a comprehensive overview of racism at varying levels in the United States, it may be a struggle to explain the cultural and organizational forces that act to create and maintain multiple kinds of racism. CRT keeps ethnicity at the core of American life. It is scholarly practice that asks students to understand the relationship between race, the judicial system and culture from a historical and political viewpoint (Delgado & Stefancic, 2001; Bell, 1993). Delgado & Stefancic further argue that critical race theory is a framework to develop insight into racialized situations, revealing how racial inequity is more impactful and lasting than is evident. The theoretical orientation of CRT is beneficial for those individuals seeking ways to address issues of race, including current and historical kinds. It will help them move beyond the activism of the Civil Rights Movement into a much more integrated, fair, and reasonable society (Bell, 1993). CRT is best regarded as a body of legal theory focusing on critical legal research and logical thinking. .

It is founded on six assumptions:

1. Storytelling is a means of communication. Marginalized individuals have poignant tales among other methods of expressing themselves. For example, using your voice or identifying your truth through proverbs, chronicles, tales, contrary stories, poems, satire, and realistic narratives are the powerful persuasion techniques used

to explain the fake importance and hypocrisy of much of civil rights legislation.

2. Racist discrimination is not an exaggeration; it is a common occurrence.

3. Elites act against racist conduct in societies only if and when it helps them.

4. Race is a social invention, not a biological one.

5. The characteristics attributed to a specific race will alter. For instance, in the era of slavery, African Americans were typically known "happy-go-lucky and childlike" to legitimize slavery, but now they are more popularly termed, "violent and illegal" to legitimize increased police invasion.

6. Individuals have conflicting personalities, i.e., they relate to more than one ethnic group and are thus influenced in more than one way by disempowerment or discrimination. We have very different lenses through which we view the universe, with the help of others.

As per Bell (1993), CRT is grounded in the more developed aspects of African American history, geography, sociology, economics, culture, theory, law, and politics. According to West (1993), concepts of social creation and the nature of race and prejudice are already-present in the work of well-known modern critical race researchers, such as Derrick Bell, Mari Matsuda, Richard Delgado, Kimberle Crenshaw, Gloria Ladson-Billings, & William Tate, and the recently developed CRT intellectuals, Adrienne Dixson, Celia Rousseau, Thandeka Chapman. The core characteristics of CRT provide a theoretical interpretation of recent legal discussion on the relevance of previous civil rights policies for the present political environment (Bell, 1993).

The early CRT writings can be linked back to Derrick Bell and Alan Freeman in the mid-1970s (Ladson-Billings, 1995). As per the Delgado (1995), both Bell and Freeman were extremely frustrated about the "snail rate" of social change in the United States. Extremely worried and shocked at the accelerated deterioration in the 1970s of the advances achieved by the Civil Rights Acts of the 1960s, Derrick Bell, a lawyer who worked as chief executive of the NAACP organization, started fashioning cases intended to alter current laws (Ladson-Billings, 1995).

Over the last ten years, many literary critics have directed their focus to white privilege (Bell, 1993). In the field of Critical White Studies (CWS), thinkers including Toni Morrison, Eric Foner, Peggy McIntosh, Andrew Hacker, Ruth Frankenberg, John Howard Griffin, David Roediger, Kathleen Neal Cleaver, Noel Ignatiev, Cherríe Moraga, Maurice Berger, and Reginald Horsman have attacked long-standing queries (Ladson-Billings, 1995).

They ask 1) How was whiteness developed, or even why? 2) Why did the definition of whiteness shift across time? 3) Why did certain ethnic communities, including the Irish and the Jews, claim to be white and turn white later on? 4) Can some individuals be white at various times, and what would it mean to be white? 5) At what stage does the privilege of being white step over the line of white superiority or white racism? And 6) What do whites who worry about existing inequalities or white supremacy do about it?

More importantly, culturally diverse subgroups have been established within field of CRT literature, including (Bell, 1995); 1) Latino Critical Race Studies; 2) Functionalist Asian Studies, and 3) Critical Race Native Studies. Currently, CRT acts as a practical platform that gives analytical insight to academics, professionals, and students searching for ways to explore topics relating to race. They want answers to past and current manifestations of oppression and culture that push far beyond the civil rights age of protest to create a much more multicultural, equal and egalitarian U.S. society.

Chapter 11: The Model Minority Myth

Model minority is a specific term used to narrate Asian Americans as a beneficial, hard-working, skilled, and lawful ethnic minority that really has overcome mental anguish, injustice and prejudice. This image also includes traits such as filial piety, and dignity of the aged amid gender and demographic hierarchies. Nevertheless, the word, model minority, is a racist interpretation forced on Asian Americans from the outside, usually by upper class whites. Asian Americans face racial biased in the United States as "immigrants" and quite often are labeled as "ethnic"— more Asian than American. They are considered to be non-native English speakers and non-citizens (as seen in the query, "Where do you come from?") "The concept of a model minority has been dominantly imposed on them irrespective of their current immigration or demographic privileges" (Tuan, 1999).

To make distinctions between Japanese Americans and African Americans, sociologist, William Petersen, initially introduced and brought into vogue the use of the word, model minority. In his 1966 New York Times Magazine story, "Success Story, Japanese-American Style," he consolidated a widespread stereotypical image of Asians (e.g. Japanese) as policy-abiding citizens who became proficient enough to rise well above the difficult circumstances of their Second World War imprisonment in confinement camps. A comparable description has been implemented for other cultural minorities of Asian American origin. Petersen 's portrayal represents a decisive shift from the conventional media representation of Asian immigrants and their children, exposing words like "apelike," "filthy," "servile," "exotic," and "risky." He made a tremendous contribution to Japanese American social traditions, good work ethics, family dynamics, and heredity that contrasted directly with the hotly debated 1965 Moynihan Report (U.S depart of labor, 1965,) which criticized African American custom and their family system for the social and financial issues they confronted in United States of America. These analogies wrongly infuse anti-Asian prejudice with anti-black racism (figure in Ancheta, 2000).

The minority model identity confirms the impression that bigotry in the United States isn't an issue any longer. It highlights the idea of the United States as having a political orientation that grants equal rights and opportunities to everybody, irrespective of race, class, sexuality, or gender - fairly rewarding the extra effort and services of citizens with financial upward development. As per this misguided assumption, it is assumed that for all those who fall behind, it is due to terrible decisions or a substandard society. This expectation affirmed the traditional deficit model that informed the Petersen and Moynihan studies, famous in the 1960s and 1970s. Even so, the concept of a model minority doesn't foster basic citizenship equalities for Asian Americans. The white-built tag does not safeguard Asian Americans from sexism and xenophobia either. Rather, it implies an "inferior category retained for specific minorities, those 'behave' adequately and remain without protest in their allocated secondary residence." In comparison, "the model minority paradigm, as a hegemonic tool, preserves the white supremacy of the social system by distracting interest from ethnic disparity and setting expectations on how immigrants will act" (Lee, 1996, p.6). It also points to Asians as the "standard" such that African-Americans, Latinos as well as other ethnic groups are "negative" minorities. Generally, as the reasoning suggests, if Asian Americans can succeed without state assistance, why can't African Americans and perhaps other communities of racial minorities? It distracts focus from institutionalized racism and social inequalities by striking minority communities against each other and impedes the appeal for social fairness for certain other racial minorities.

Assimilationist immigration transition systems strengthen the idea of a minority paradigm. Traditional assimilation studies postulate that from each subsequent generation in the host state, immigrants and their descendants slowly leave their old organizational and social habits as they learn new beliefs and attitudes, thereby doing the same as whites. It even further indicates that "there is a gradual cycle through which different ethnic groups tend to share a shared community and achieve fair opportunities to society's resources system." Even so, assimilationist ideas fail to realize the recipient society's numerous cultural and spatial restraints that drastically reduce equal rights and opportunities for racial minorities. Theorists in assimilation, focusing on the social success of Asian Americans (e.g., gains in employment and income), have proposed that Asian Americans are on track to accomplish real acceptance into U.S. society. It also means that Asian

Americans are excluded from racial injustice, prejudice and other types of injustice encounters and have "done it" in U.S. culture. That's far from the living reality and the socioeconomic conditions of Asian Americans. With the initial arrival of Chinese immigrants throughout the mid-nineteenth century, Asian Americans faced bigotry and prejudice in working in California's mining companies and while building the interstate highway system. Their sheer number and job practices led to the nationalist sentiment that viewed them as the "yellow peril," a derogatory word used to define East Asian citizens as a threat to the Western world. Congress passed a series of discriminatory legislation that prevented Asians from entering the U.S. between the 1880s through the 1920s. It wasn't until 1965, with the approval of the 1965 Immigration and Nationality Act, that constraints on Asian immigration were finally removed.

The myth of the minority model often operates as a theoretical construct. This tag form affects how people accept Asian Americans as well as how they approach themselves and their ethnic others. In keeping with the way violence works, Asian Americans rationalize an authenticity that mimics the pictures forced on them by the more powerful group (for example, the model minority). They recognize and realize the attitudes and misconceptions regarding everyone's group. This generates enormous stress for Asian Americans to integrate themselves into white-dominated traditions and comply to with own white-defined visuals. This conceptualization may have damaging consequences on the self-concepts and psychological wellbeing of Asian Americans, explained by Osajima (1993) as "the concealed problems of race," even though there are no active situations of prejudice.

Demographic profile

The very first step towards the dissolution of the model minority concept is to illustrate the inclusiveness within and throughout the groups classified as Asian Americans. Asian Americans appear to have reached cultural and financial equality with their European American predecessors, as shown by a closer analysis of disaggregated quantitative information on Asian American subgroups. They include differentiated longitudinal data on identified Asian American subgroups, concentrating on their level of achievement in higher education, jobs, average household personal income and property, deprivation and access to medical care. We use data analysis for the Asian Americans and Pacific Islanders (AAPI information) to gain demographic data and an appropriate strategy.

Higher education

Academic attainment is a major contributor to the view of Asian Americans as a marginalized model. As a community, Asian Americans appear to have accomplished good academic achievement in the United States. About 50.5 percent of all those who are recognized as Asian (alone and in confluence) having gotten higher than a bachelor's degree (especially in comparison to 33.2 percent of whites and 29.8 percent of the overall U.S. population). The rising academic accomplishment of Asian Americans is often directly linked to their history and culture (e.g. Confucianism) along with their standard of education (which includes parental care in children's education and an emphasis on success). Even so, a closer study shows that educational success ranges greatly across Asian subgroups.

Country Name	**Higher Education Percentage**
Taiwanese	(75.3%)
Asian Indian	(71.3%)
Mongolian	(60.2%)
Sri Lankan	(57.5%)
Malaysian	(56.2%)
Burmese	(25.7%)
Cambodian	(17.0%)

Hmong	(16.7%)
Laotian	(14.5%)
Bhutanese	(13.9%)

Employment

Asian Americans are desirable in a broad range of fields, but seem to be considered best in management, professional careers, and relevant professions more than most other ethnic groups. (About fifty percent of Asian Americans work in sectors correlated with thirty eight percent of the state average, thirty nine percent of whites, twenty percent of Latinos, and twenty nine percent of African Americans.) Yet in their jobs, Asian Americans tend to face bigotry and prejudice. Research has examined the 5 largest groups in Asia (Chinese, Indians, Philippines, Vietnamese, and Koreans) identified as being unique. The so-called "Asian second generation benefit" in academic performance is not always transferred to the labor force of all future Asians, except for the Chinese. In Fortune five hundred companies, Asian Americans consist of only two percent of executives and three percent of department members, while blacks and Latinos hold eight and four percent of Fortune five hundred corporate board seats. Asian Americans are severely underrepresented in specific roles in consulting firms, and public sector and academic institutions, even though they have become part of every sector. Furthermore, the research showed that Asian American lawyers report institutional racism and misconceptions or stereotypes as barriers to better employment or advancement, with female Asian American lawyers considerably more likely to actively encounter race-based discrimination. Despite having been the major indigenous population of workers in Silicon Valley's tech sector, Asian Americans were much less able to become supervisors and executives among all races, with Asian women the least likely group to become managers. In academics, related phenomena were found.

Asian Americans and Pacific Islanders (AAPI) make up ten percent of all full-time faculty (six percent male and four percent female) relative to seventy-six percent male and thirty-five percent female of their white colleagues (National Center for Education Estimates, 2017) as seen by assessing one and half million faculty members in higher academic institutions through the summer of 2016.

Of full-time adjunct professors, seven percent were male and AAPI while six percent were females and AAPI. Even so, the number of Asian American females fell as they advanced in college grades and qualified at only three percent of full-time professors. Asian Americans generally have a greater labor-force participation percentage than the state average, and they have continuously had the lowest joblessness percentage of any ethnic group up to 2010. Among the homeless, Asian Americans are amongst those with the maximum joblessness period (similar to African Americans). In 2013, forty-two percent of the jobless Asian American public experienced it long-term (for example, twenty-seven weeks or more) contrasted with thirty-six percent of jobless white and thirty-five percent of jobless Latinos.

Poverty

Asian Americans have the lowest rates of poverty amongst ethnic minority groups. (Thirteen percent of Asians were living in poverty especially in comparison to sixteen percent of the overall U.S. overall, eleven percent of whites, twenty-four percent of Hispanics / Latinos, and twenty-seven percent of African Americans). In relation to child poverty, Asian Americans (thirteen percent) now have the least percentage compared with children of other ethnicities (seventeen pe cent of whites, thirty-three percent of Latinos, thirty-nine percent of African Americans and twenty-two percent as the state average). The rate of poverty for the elderly (i.e. age of sixty-five or older) presented a quite different and distressing picture. Asian American senior citizens have a relatively high level of poverty at thirteen percent (especially in comparison to eight percent of whites and nine percent as the state median). Moreover, data from 2007 to 2011 indicate that Asian Americans have been the fastest-growing population in a condition poverty since the Great Recession, increasing by sixty percent, far greater than any other racial group, and exceeding the national rise by twenty-seven percent (Ramakrishnan & Ahmad, 2014).

National Origin Groups	**Poverty Percentage**
Highest levels of their populations living below the federal poverty line	
Burmese	(37.8%)
Bhutanese	(34.3%)
Nepalese	(26.1%)
Hmong	(26.1%)
Mongolian	(25.1%)
Lowest levels of their population living below the federal line	
Taiwanese	(12.2%)
Sri Lankan	(10.9%)
Japanese	(8.8%)
Asian Indian	(8.1%)
Filipino	(7.9%)

Review of relevant literature

Compatible with the Social Justice model and the Critical Race Feminist Theory, the aim of this paper is to highlight how one's social location could differentiate personal perspective, making viewable structural and concealed discrepancies within varying Asian racial groups, and classifying social contexts and legitimizing oppression and entitlement. We present a literature review on the responsibilities of families within a community's context and based on the condition of socialization of Asian Americans in the field of academic achievement, gender, psychological adaptation, and mental wellbeing. Considering the increasing population of Asian Americans in the United States, any study on Asian American families remains elusive, and not all racial subgroups are described in published studies (Fang et al., 2008). Also when Asian American families are researched, almost all of the research using the interview method focuses on the racial group as an absolute term without attempting to make racial differences. Others who have studied particular ethnicities do so mainly with a focus on Chinese American families.

Conclusion

The progress we want on anti-racism is now on the rise. The word is spreading, and perhaps racism can be easily dismantled by providing guidance to children and young people so they can see what is inaccurate and what is appropriate in regard those who are distinct from them. This study offers a summary of possible educational activities by federal and provincial governments. Anti-racism education has become a known requirement for youth. There is every justification to be convinced that these and other preceding attempts have increased performance and effectiveness, so that the messages and practices of racists will progressively fall on deaf ears. The objective is to look back and learn as a basic requirement for meaningful thinking to foster improvement and adjustment for those guided by standards of quality and legislature.

The lessons learned from experience are systematic and indicative of the road to come in the drive for cultural and legal reform. Even though civil and democratic freedoms are being compromised in an effort to assimilate, incorporate and integrate "in pursuit of a smooth, colorless, etiolated homogeneity, founded on the changing sands of assimilation and focused on changing values. Encouraging positive strategies will be a complicated process that continues to inspire the anti-racist social work by activists who desire to enhance individual and group identity and also the usefulness of cultural context in anti-racist practice. Political ideology remains a major influence for many people who are particularly worried about the concept of black and white superiority that leads to racism.

We can't let ourselves get mentally clogged up in specificities. We need to have an international viewpoint, as well as one focused on local and national issues. We have to think about moving from the specific to the general and the general to the specific, both of at the same time. Then we can effectively turn individual instances into cultural archetypes, cultural issues into community causes, and community causes into national movements. Thus, the anti-racist movement has a reliable history of motivating individuals and groups who have taken collective decisions to accomplish important political objectives that utilize an evaluated methodology.

Much positive changes and development has already occurred, but much more has to be done to engage those with additional perspectives, such as service users, students, and others who make societal, religious and ethnic distinctions. The significance of interpretation and categorization is essential, and words that are efficiently analyzed before use can lead to a radical progress in comprehension. Eventually, it may become necessary for professionals to consider how best to quickly and effectively promote an anti-racist strategy in a dedicated and enthusiastic way to motivate trainees and new graduate social workers. Even though language improvements have been a significant moment for anti-racist practice, such a discussion demands a move towards a mutual understanding of communication and its influence on communal civilization.

It is also worth considering undertaking a deeper study of how societies actually live together. Some individuals, for example, live comfortably in parallel societies, sharing similar views on culture, religion, ideology, traditions, and common lifestyles, while others experience a great deal of trouble in this regard.

In fact, there is considerable evidence to conclude that human contact is often referred to as common and reciprocal empathy instead of personal distance and confrontation. These points should provide the reader with the ability to synthesize lessons from this book on a number of issues revolving around racism and cultural variations, prompting solutions that include, rather than exempt, individuals and communities.

CPSIA information can be obtained
at www.ICGtesting.com
Printed in the USA
LVHW012333060820
662581LV00005B/1532